Graphic Organizers Across the Curriculum
Grade Five

W9-BJS-738

Table of Contents

Graphic Organizers Across the Curriculum
Grade Five

Introduction

Graphic organizers are tools for learning that allow students to see on paper what they may have trouble thinking through in their minds. Graphic organizers present a clear, visual picture of a concept or measurement that gives students a unique opportunity not only to grasp the concept presented but also to move beyond it toward understanding related concepts. Graphic organizers help students to see relationships, to structure thinking, to remember vocabulary, facts, and concepts, and to acquire and apply their skills and knowledge. *Graphic Organizers Across the Curriculum* provides teachers with reproducible materials to help students gain this knowledge through interpreting, using, and creating a variety of graphic organizers.

Students' learning and teachers' effectiveness today are assessed through national standards. Standards across the curriculum require that students be able to read, interpret, and use graphic organizers of all kinds in every subject area. Students are often expected to interpret information in graphic organizers on standardized tests.

Organization

This book is organized into six units: Charts and Tables, Diagrams, Graphs, Lines, Maps, and Language and Memory Aids. Within each category are several kinds of graphic organizers. First, there is a blank graphic organizer that can be used to fit a variety of lesson plans. These blank organizers can be used with the activities in this book or with your own classroom activities. Then, there is a completed example of each graphic organizer. These examples are indicated by the icon ◑ in the upper right corner and are meant to give students a clearer picture of how the graphic organizer can be used. Finally, there are exercise pages, indicated by the icon ◑, using the graphic organizer. The exercise pages can be used to supplement your curriculum and give your students the opportunity to use and interpret

graphic organizers. The directions indicate which blank graphic organizer to reproduce and provide to students.

Icons representing curriclum areas are shown at the bottom right of each example and lesson page. These icons are also shown on the Correlation to Curriculum/Student Pages on page 5. The icons will assist you in integrating these lessons into your lesson plans.

There is a Letter to Parents on page 6. Talk about the letter with your students, and send it home to enhance communication and understanding between parents and the school.

Use

The lessons in this book are meant to supplement your curriculum. It is assumed that the students will have some familiarity with graphic organizers or prior instruction before completing these pages. They can be given to students to work on individually or in pairs, or they can be used as a center activity. It is recommended that you go over each exercise with students before they begin. Discussion about the correct usage and completion of the graphic organizers is important to your students' understanding and success with the exercises.

Assign only one page at a time. Be sure that students understand each type of graphic organizer before moving on. If a student is having difficulty, use a blank graphic organizer to create a simpler one of the same type. Review the pages after the students have completed their work. Encourage discussion about the activities.

Display completed worksheets to show students' progress. The goal should be for students to be familiar and comfortable with graphic organizers, so that as they move forward, they will know how to use them and will be able to concentrate on the information they contain, not on the organizers themselves.

Graphic organizers can bring fun, excitement, and color into the classroom. Have fun, and your students will, too!

Acronyms

Acronyms, or acrostics, can be used to help students remember words or the order of words by creating a new word or phrase that is easy to remember. The word or phrase usually has no connection to the words being remembered; it is simply easier to recall. An acronym can be used in any content area. When students make up their own acronyms, they will be even more likely to remember them.

Here are some commonly used acronyms:

Social Studies
The compass points:

N	Never
E	Eat
S	Sour
W	Watermelons

The Great Lakes:

H	Huron
O	Ontario
M	Michigan
E	Erie
S	Superior

Math
An order of operations:

M	My	(Multiplication)
D	Dear	(Division)
A	Aunt	(Addition)
S	Sally	(Subtraction)

or for older students:

P	Please	(Parentheses)
E	Excuse	(Exponents)
M	My	(Multiplication)
D	Dear	(Division)
A	Aunt	(Addition)
S	Sally	(Subtraction)

or:

P	Parentheses
E	Exponents
M	Multiplication
D	Division
A	Addition
S	Subtraction

Science
The order of the planets from the Sun:

Mercury	My
Venus	Very
Earth	Efficient
Mars	Mother
Jupiter	Just
Saturn	Served
Uranus	Us
Neptune	Nine
Pluto	Pizzas!

The order of the colors in a prism, or the rainbow (said like a man's name):

R	Red
O	Orange
Y	Yellow
G.	Green
B	Blue
I	Indigo
V	Violet

Music
The notes on a musical scale:

FACE, and

E	Every	or	Every
G	Good		Good
B	Boy		Boy
D	Does		Deserves
F	Fine		Fudge

Other Mnemonic Strategies

Mnemonic strategies help students remember facts and information. It is important to note that while these strategies help students to recall facts, they may not ensure that students understand what the facts mean. However, using some of the following methods to help students remember will set a foundation on which they can build further learning.

Some things to remember when using mnemonic strategies are:

- That they be meaningful—for example, if a song is used, it should be one that the students are already familiar with and that students at that age would know.

- That they be interesting—visuals should be colorful and draw students' attention.

- That they be repeated—bring students' attention back to the rhyme, picture, or object often, until students think of it naturally. These devices require remembering, too, but they should be easier to recall because they are fun, unique, and meaningful to the students.

The following are examples of some commonly used mnemonic strategies.

Rhyming and Songs

Some rhymes have been part of our learning for many years. Two examples are: The alphabet song, "ABCDEFG…," and "*i* before *e*, except after *c*, or when it says *a* as in *neighbor* and *weigh*."
Of course, we all remember this rhyme: "Columbus sailed the ocean blue in fourteen hundred ninety-two."

A popular song to help social studies students remember the continents goes to the tune of "London Bridge": "North and South America,/Asia,/Africa,/ Europe and Australia,/and Antarctica!"

Fun Stories

Funny stories can be created around a list of words to help students remember. If you have a list of vocabulary words, for example, students can write the list on a piece of paper. Then, they can build a silly story around the words. Remembering the story will be easy for them, and the words will all be there!

Chunking

Learning information in chunks, or groups of similar things, helps students remember large amounts of information. Rather than remembering all types of trees, for example, students can divide the trees into subgroups. The groups may include deciduous, evergreen, and conifer trees. Students can see how the members of each group are alike and how each group is like or different from the other groups. When learning the history of another culture, the culture can be broken down into subgroups such as food, clothing, transportation, government, and customs. These smaller groups can then be put together into a meaningful picture of the way life used to be.

Visuals

Giving students a picture to remember will help them recall information and concepts. Visual imagery, hand-in-hand with the subject matter, has always had an impact on students' learning. Pictures give students something more tangible to remember and give more meaning to an unfamiliar word or concept.

Concrete Objects

Artifacts, costumes, and representations (such as props) may all be used. Students not only have a chance to see the object but can use other senses. When studying the Far East, students could smell and taste spices. They could compare foods with and without spices. Touching, smelling, and tasting objects, as well as seeing them, will have an impact that hearing about things alone can never have. Representations, such as three cardboard ships for Columbus' journey, will reinforce the learning of that lesson.

Correlation to Curriculum/Student Pages

Page	Social Studies	Science & Health	Language Arts	Math	History
8			X		X
9	X		X		
11	X				
12	X				
14		X			
15		X	X		
17				X	
18				X	
20				X	
21				X	
23				X	
24				X	
26		X	X		
27			X		X
29			X		
30			X		
31			X		
33		X			
34		X			
36		X	X		
37		X	X	X	
39		X	X		
40			X		
42			X		X
43			X		X
45		X	X		
46		X	X		
48			X		
49			X		
51				X	
52				X	
54		X	X		
55		X	X		
57			X		X
58			X		X
60			X		X
61		X	X		X
63				X	
64				X	
66				X	
67				X	
69				X	
70	X			X	
72		X		X	
73		X		X	
75				X	
76				X	
78	X			X	
79		X		X	
81					X
82				X	X
84				X	
85	X				
86	X				X
87	X				
88	X				
89	X				X
91		X	X		X
93			X		
94			X		

Dear Parent,

During this school year, our class will be integrating graphic organizers into our curriculum. These organizers—charts and tables, diagrams, time lines, maps, and memory aids—will help your child to acquire the skills necessary to do well on standard assessments. Graphic organizers are an important part of your child's learning in every subject at school. In the fifth grade, our goal is improve students' skills with many different types of graphic organizers and to have students practice interpreting and creating graphic organizers. Students are also introduced to some of the more complex graphic organizers that they will be using in higher grades.

From time to time, I may send activity sheets home. Please be assured that these exercises have been discussed in class and that I feel the students are familiar enough with the exercises to work independently. To help your child do his or her best work, please consider the following suggestions:

• Provide a quiet place to work.
• Go over the worksheet together. This will help your child to focus on the lesson and remember what was discussed in class.
• Encourage your child to do his or her best.
• Check the lesson when it is complete. Note improvements as well as problems.
• Let your child know that "best effort" is all that is required. If your child is having problems with the exercise after trying his or her best, we will address them in class.

Help your child maintain a positive attitude about graphic organizers. They can add interest and fun to schoolwork, and should be considered a challenge, but not a chore. Enjoy this time you spend with your child. With your support, graphic organizers will become useful, important tools in your child's education.

Thank you for your support.

Sincerely,

Name _____

Date _____

K What do I **KNOW**?	W What do I **WANT** to know?	H **HOW** will I learn?	L What did I **LEARN**?

K What do I **KNOW**?	W What do I **WANT** to know?	H **HOW** will I learn?	L What did I **LEARN**?
There are many large, historic homes in my town. I know that my town was a busy seaport at one time.	I would like to know what types of commerce thrived in my town in the early 1900s. I would like to know what attracted people to live and do business in my town.	I will research books about the history of my town. I will go to the Historical Society and the town museum to study the exhibits and to talk to the people who work there. I will go to my town's Internet site.	I discovered that many of the old homes in my town were once surrounded by farmland. The ports were very busy because that is how the people got much of the food and supplies that they needed. Also, there was a thriving shipbuilding industry. Some of the historical homes once belonged to sea captains.

Near and Far

A **KWHL chart** helps you to focus on what you want to learn. First, you think of something you would like to know more about. Then, in the **K** column, you write what you already know. In the **W** column, you write what you want to know. In the **H** column, you tell how you will find the information. In the **L** column, you write what you have learned.

Directions Choose one of these activities. Use the blank KWHL chart on page 7 to complete the activity.

Activity 1:

What do you know about your own town or city? What would you like to know? Fill in the **K**, **W**, and **H** columns in the chart, research to find the answers to your questions, and fill in the **L** column.

Activity 2:

Learn more about your own state or another state that interests you. Choose a state. Fill in the **K**, **W**, and **H** columns in the chart, research to find the answers to your questions, and fill in the **L** column.

Activity 3:

Do you ever wonder what life is like in other countries? What country would you like to know more about? Choose another country to learn about. Fill in the **K**, **W**, and **H** columns in the chart, research to find the answers to your questions, and fill in the **L** column.

Cool!

Create a piece of art to go with your KWHL chart. You can use photographs, paint or draw a picture, make a collage, or build a three-dimensional object. Your artwork should illustrate something that you learned by completing the chart.

DiPietro Family Chores

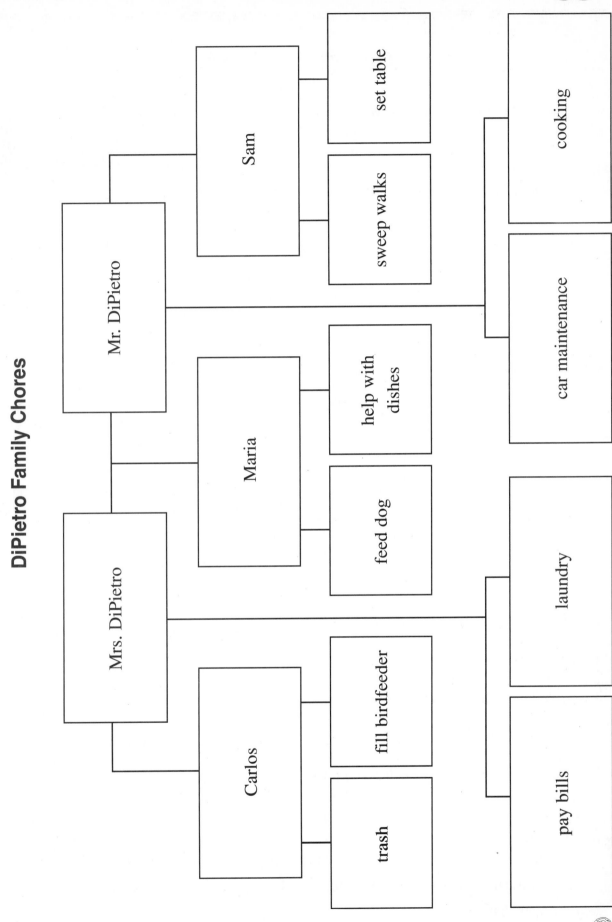

www.svschoolsupply.com
© Steck-Vaughn Company

Charts & Tables: Organizational Chart
Graphic Organizers Across the Curriculum 5, SV 3418-5

Get Organized

An **organizational chart** shows how a group, business, or government is set up. It is a way of organizing responsibilities.

Directions Use this organizational chart to answer questions 1–4.

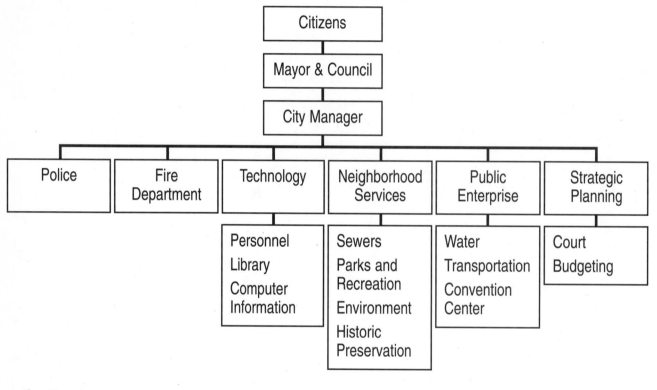

1. To whom are the mayor and council responsible? _____

2. To whom is the fire department directly responsible? _____

3. According to this chart, who is directly responsible for historic preservation of the city?

_____

4. Which city department provides computer information? _____

Cool!

Use the blank worksheet on page 10 to make an organizational chart for your family. If the blank worksheet does not work well for your family, use it as a guide to make your own chart.

DiPietro Family Chores

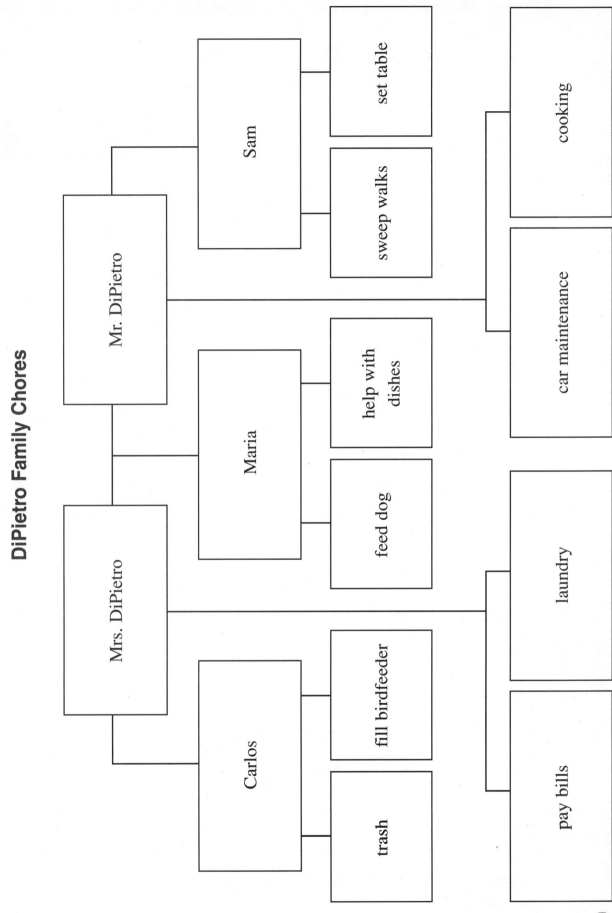

Mr. DiPietro

- Sam
  - set table
  - sweep walks
- car maintenance
- cooking

Mrs. DiPietro

- Maria
  - help with dishes
  - feed dog
- Carlos
  - fill birdfeeder
  - trash
- laundry
- pay bills

Get Organized

An **organizational chart** shows how a group, business, or government is set up. It is a way of organizing responsibilities.

Directions Use this organizational chart to answer questions 1–4.

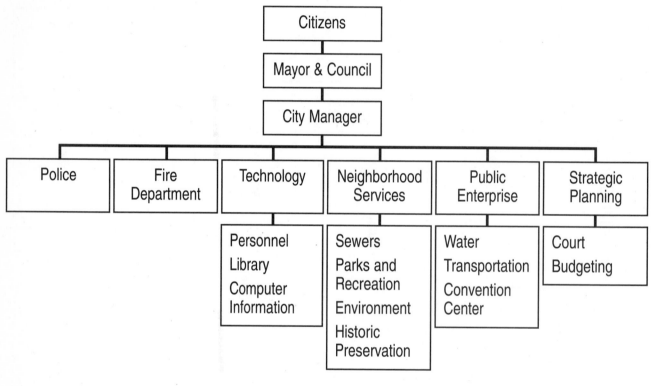

1. To whom are the mayor and council responsible? _____

2. To whom is the fire department directly responsible? _____

3. According to this chart, who is directly responsible for historic preservation of the city?

_____

4. Which city department provides computer information? _____

Cool!

Use the blank worksheet on page 10 to make an organizational chart for your family. If the blank worksheet does not work well for your family, use it as a guide to make your own chart.

Date _____

Name _____

Characteristics

Things to Compare

Characteristics			
	Place to Play	**Equipment**	**Number of Players**
Basketball	Court (indoors or outdoors)	Basket(s) 1 Ball	1 to 5 on each team
Tennis	Court (indoors or outdoors)	Net Racket 2 or 3 Balls	1 or 2 on each team
Soccer	Field (indoors or outdoors)	1 Soccer Ball Nets	11 on each team
Football	Field (outdoors)	1 Football Goals	11 on each team

Things to Compare (left vertical label)

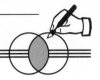

Animals Adapt

Animals have different ways to adapt to their environments so they can survive in winter. You can see how animals are alike or different by using a chart, or matrix.

Directions Use the blank compare and contrast matrix on page 13. Enter the following information into the matrix.

Animals to Compare:
Bear
Whale
Snowshoe Rabbit
Canada Goose
Monarch Butterfly

Characteristics:
Migrate
Hibernate
Camouflage

Find out which characteristic fits each animal. Complete the chart by writing *yes* or *no* under each characteristic. Then, answer the questions.

1. What does a whale do in the winter? _____

2. How does a snowshoe rabbit protect itself in the winter? _____

3. Which animal hibernates in the winter? _____

4. What three animals move to a warmer place in the winter? _____

_____

5. How does camouflage help an animal to survive in winter? If you don't know, find out.

_____

_____

Cool!

Choose five other animals. Use another blank matrix to compare and contrast three characteristics. You may use the same characteristics that are on the chart above, or choose your own.

Name _____

Date _____

Charts & Tables: Logic Table
Graphic Organizers Across the Curriculum 5, SV 3418-5

Using Logic

What is each person's favorite food? Each person is different. Use what you **do** know to find out what you **do not** know.

- Carlos does not like tomato sauce. There is an **X** under Pizza and Spaghetti for Carlos.

- Aisha loves tacos. It says **yes** under tacos for Aisha, and there are **X's** under Pizza, Chicken Fingers, and Spaghetti.

- Jeff's favorite restaurant is Pinky's Pizza House. So, it says **yes** under Pizza for Jeff, and there are **X's** under Tacos, Chicken Fingers, and Spaghetti.

Favorite Foods

Name	Pizza	Tacos	Chicken Fingers	Spaghetti
Carlos	X			X
Aisha	X	Yes	X	X
Jeff	Yes	X	X	X
Jessica				

Now what do you know?

- Tacos are Aisha's favorite food. So tacos cannot be Carlos' favorite food. Put an **X** under Tacos for Carlos. His favorite food must be Chicken Fingers, so write **yes** under Chicken Fingers for Carlos.

- To find Jessica's favorite food, put an **X** in the boxes that show Carlos', Aisha's, and Jeff's favorite foods. The box left over is Spaghetti. So write **yes** under Spaghetti for Jessica.

Charts & Tables: Logic Table
Graphic Organizers Across the Curriculum 5, SV 3418-5

That Makes Sense

A **logic table** can help you find an answer when you don't have all the facts.

Directions Use the blank logic tables on page 16 to complete the following exercises.

1. Donna, Li, Sari, and Evita belong to different sports teams. One is on the swim team, one is on the softball team, one is on the basketball team, and one is on the track team. Who is on which team?

This is what you know:

Li and Evita are afraid of the water.

Sari forgot her catcher's mitt at practice.

Evita won the 100-meter dash.

2. Mari, Kiran, Bryan, and Kim are all going on vacation. Everyone is going somewhere. But no two people are going to the same place. One will take a cruise to the island of Bermuda, one will fly to California, one will ride a train to Canada, and one will drive to New York City. Who is going where?

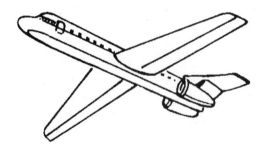

This is what you know:

Mari won't go to California.

Kiran wants to go to an island.

Bryan doesn't want to fly.

Kim wants to see the Pacific Ocean.

Bryan wants to see the largest city in the United States.

Cool!

Make a logic table of your own. Think of clues for all but one of the subjects on your table. Test your clues to be sure they make sense. Then, get a blank table and trade clues and blank tables with a classmate.

Name _____ Date _____

X	2	4	6	8	10	12	14	16	18	20
2	4	8	12	16	20	24	28	32	36	40
4	8	16	24	32	40	48	56	64	72	80
6	12	24	36	48	60	72	84	96	108	120
8	16	32	48	64	80	96	112	128	144	160
10	20	40	60	80	100	120	140	160	180	200
12	24	48	72	96	120	144	168	192	216	240
14	28	56	84	112	140	168	196	224	252	280
16	32	64	96	128	160	192	224	256	288	320
18	36	72	108	144	180	216	252	288	324	360
20	40	80	120	160	200	240	280	320	360	400

Charts & Tables: Math Grid
Graphic Organizers Across the Curriculum 5, SV 3418-5

Table Talk

A **math grid** can help you with multiplication and division problems. This math grid is for multiples of 3.

 Use the grid to solve the problems below.

X	3	6	9	12	15	18	21	24	27	30
3	9	18	27	36	45	54	63	72	81	90
6	18	36	54	72	90	108	126	144	162	180
9	27	54	81	108	135	162	189	216	243	270
12	36	72	108	144	180	216	252	288	324	360
15	45	90	135	180	225	270	315	360	405	450
18	54	108	162	216	270	324	378	432	486	540
21	63	126	189	252	315	378	441	504	567	630
24	72	144	216	288	360	432	504	576	648	720
27	81	162	243	324	405	486	567	648	729	810
30	90	180	270	360	450	540	630	720	810	900

1. $27 \times 9 =$ **2.** $6 \times 18 =$ **3.** $441 \div 21 =$ **4.** $630 \div 30 =$

_____   _____   _____   _____

5. $135 \div 9 =$ **6.** $162 \div 18 =$ **7.** $18 \times 30 =$ **8.** $12 \times 27 =$

_____   _____   _____   _____

9. $6 \times 12 =$ **10.** $27 \times 3 =$ **11.** $432 \div 18 =$ **12.** $144 \div 12 =$

_____   _____   _____   _____

Cool!

Use the blank math grid on page 19 to make a 5's table. Write 6 problems for your table, and trade tables and problems with a classmate.

Name _____ Date _____

	Day			
Time				

Ming's Summer Schedule

	8:00–9:00	9:00–10:00	10:00–11:00	11:00–12:00	1:00–2:00	2:00–3:00	3:00–4:00
Monday	Feed/water horses		Tennis lesson			Exercise horses	
Tuesday	Feed/water horses			Babysit for Mrs. Rodriguez			Volunteer at library
Wednesday	Feed/water horses		Tennis lesson			Exercise horses	
Thursday	Feed/water horses			Babysit for Mrs. Rodriguez			Volunteer at library
Friday	Feed/water horses		Tennis lesson			Exercise horses	

Train Schedule from Milltown

Leave	Destination	Arrive
8:00 A.M.	Carson	9:40 A.M.
9:45 A.M.	Union	10:15 A.M.
10:15 A.M.	Cortland	12:10 P.M.
11:05 A.M.	Tysonville	11:35 A.M.
12:40 P.M.	Barkston	1:50 P.M.
2:50 P.M.	Vaschon	3:45 P.M.
3:00 P.M.	Appleton	5:15 P.M.
4:20 P.M.	Mellville	6:45 P.M.

Arrive on Time

Flights from Columbia, EST

Time of Departure	Destination	Time of Arrival
11:05 A.M.	Cincinnati	1:15 P.M.
11:45 A.M.	Miami	1:15 P.M.
11:58 A.M.	Chicago	2:11 P.M.
12:10 P.M.	St. Louis	2:45 P.M.
12:46 P.M.	Miami	2:16 P.M.
1:15 P.M.	New York	2:10 P.M.
1:34 P.M.	Miami	3:05 P.M.
2:00 P.M.	Buffalo	3:24 P.M.

Directions Use the schedule to answer the questions.

1. Which flight takes the least amount of time? _____

2. What time does the latest flight to Miami depart? _____

3. What is the destination of the longest flight from Columbia? _____

How long is the flight? _____

4. Aki wants to get to Miami as soon as possible, but she can't get to the airport in time for the 11:45 A.M. flight. If she takes the next flight, what time will she get to Miami? _____

5. Alex is on his way to the airport to pick up a friend who is arriving at 2:11 P.M.

Where does Alex live? _____

Cool!

Create a schedule for your week. Include chores, homework, play, and sports. Use the blank schedule at the top of page 22.

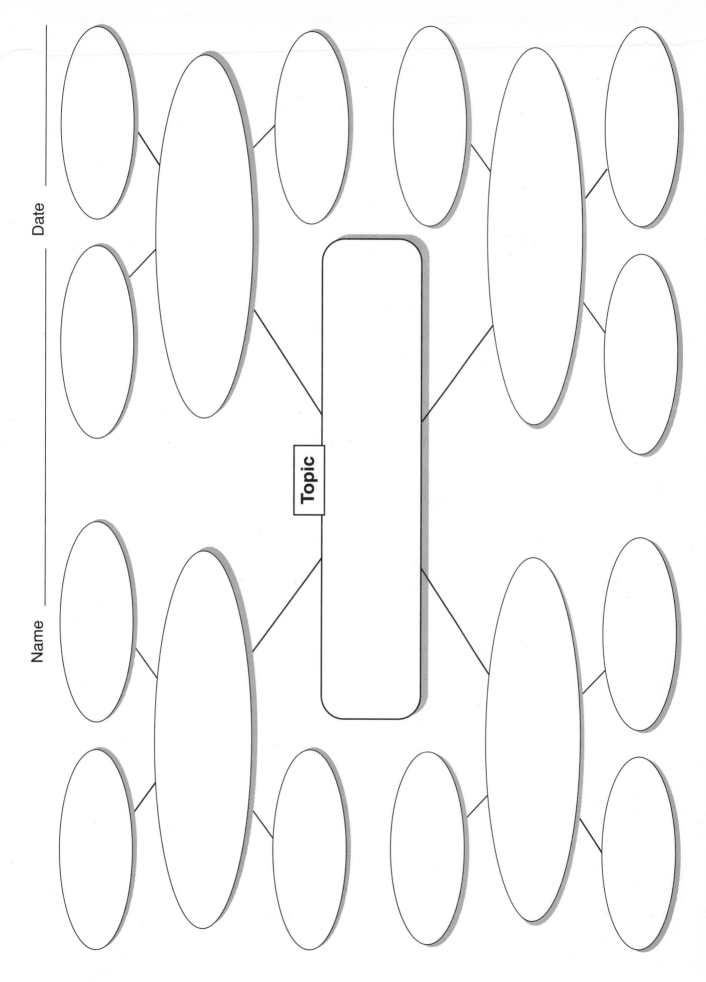

Topic

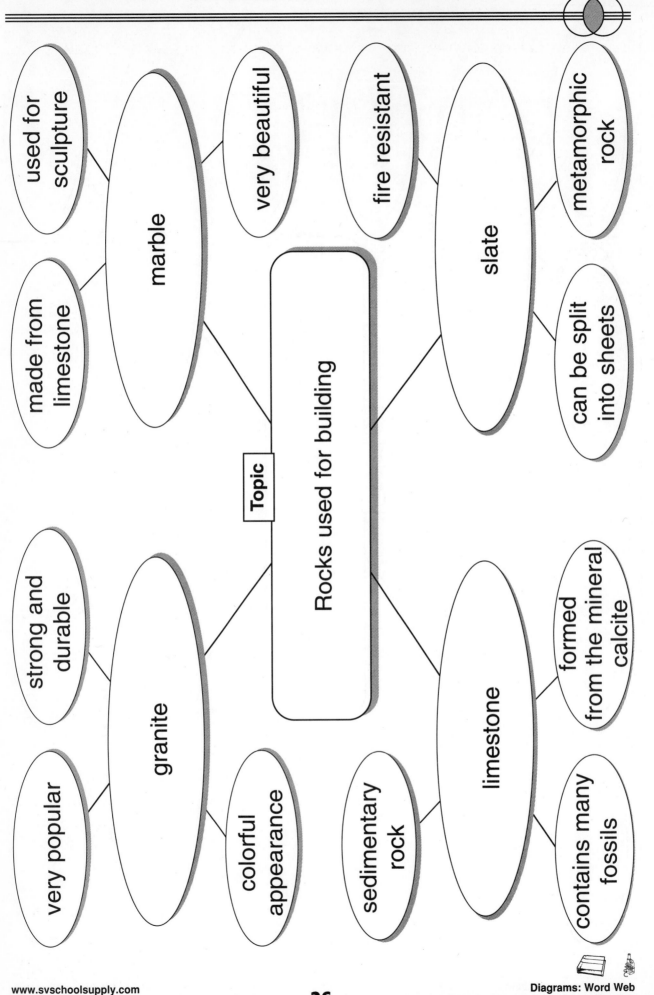

Topic

Rocks used for building

used for sculpture

very beautiful

fire resistant

metamorphic rock

marble

slate

made from limestone

can be split into sheets

strong and durable

formed from the mineral calcite

granite

limestone

very popular

colorful appearance

sedimentary rock

contains many fossils

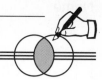

Way to Go!

A **word web** is a good way to sort information.

Directions Choose one the following groups of people. Research to find out three facts about each person. Decide what all of the people in the group have in common and write this in the Topic box of the blank word web on page 25. Use the information you found in your research to complete the web.

1. Galileo Galilei
   Thomas Edison
   Robert Goddard
   Samuel Morse

2. Jackie Joyner-Kersee
   Michelle Kwan
   Mia Hamm
   Sheryl Swoopes

3. Martin Luther King, Jr.
   Rosa Parks
   Jackie Robinson
   Fannie Lou Hamer

4. Marco Polo
   Mary Kingsley
   Amerigo Vespucci
   Sir Henry Morton Stanley

Cool!

Use the information in your word web to write a paragraph about the people that you researched.

_____

_____

_____

_____

_____

_____

_____

Name _____ Date _____

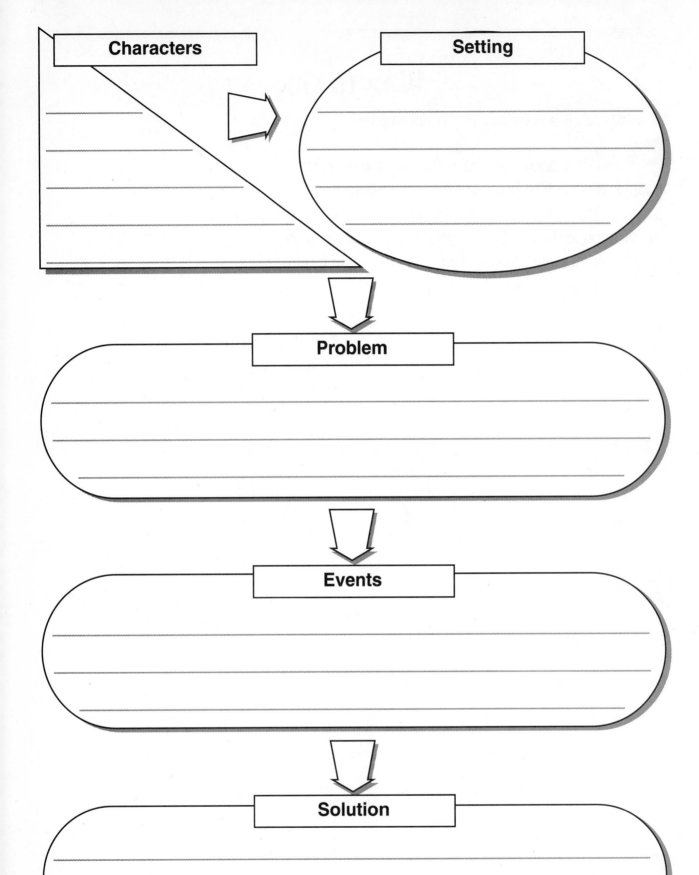

Characters

Setting

Problem

Events

Solution

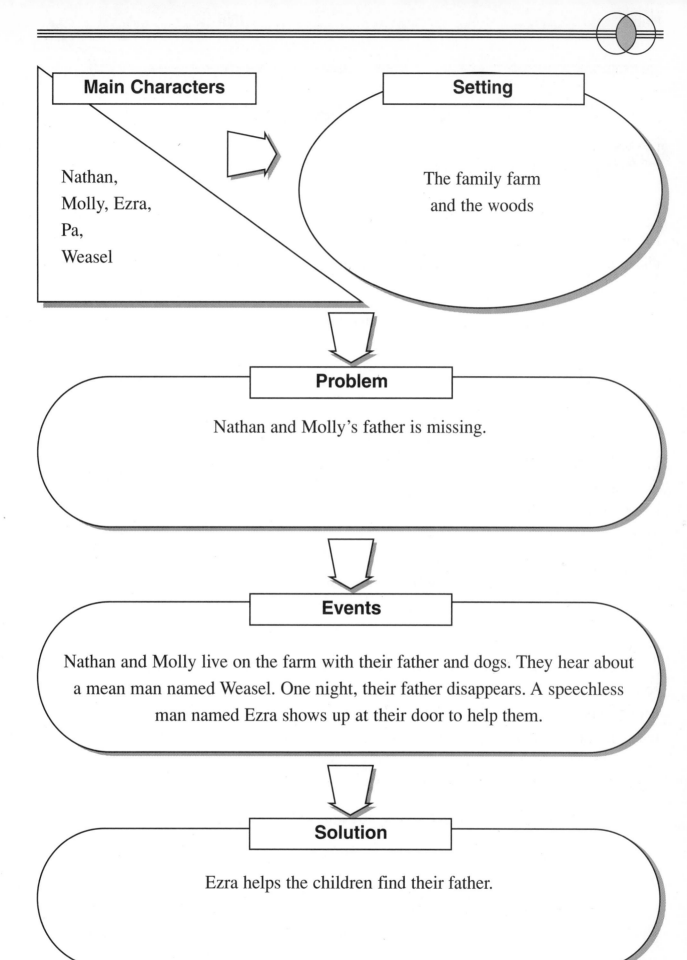

Main Characters

Nathan,
Molly, Ezra,
Pa,
Weasel

Setting

The family farm
and the woods

Problem

Nathan and Molly's father is missing.

Events

Nathan and Molly live on the farm with their father and dogs. They hear about
a mean man named Weasel. One night, their father disappears. A speechless
man named Ezra shows up at their door to help them.

Solution

Ezra helps the children find their father.

Taking a Load Off

 Read the story. Then, use it to complete the blank story map on page 28.

Carmen's mother walked in the door and collapsed on the sofa, rubbed her fingers across her forehead, and sat still for a moment. Soon, she got up and went into the kitchen to begin dinner preparations. "Carmen," she called. "Would you please come out here and empty the dishwasher?"

"Oh, Mom!" moaned Carmen. "I always have to empty the dishwasher. Why do I have to do everything?"

Her mother put her head around the corner and glared at Carmen. "You do everything? I want you to think about that one."

Carmen got up and began unloading the dishwasher and putting the dishes in the cupboards. What was her mother angry about? Carmen did unload the dishwasher a lot—not always, but a lot. She looked at her mother out of the corner of her eye. She did look tired; she was rubbing her back, and she moved slowly. She must have had a difficult day; she was on her feet most of the time at the store. Suddenly Carmen thought of a way that she could help her mother to feel better, and she waited for the next day with anticipation.

When Carmen got home from school the next afternoon, she straightened the house and got some things from the cupboard for a simple dinner. She went to her mother's room and found her slippers, heated some water for tea, and put a tea bag in a cup. When her mother walked in the door, Carmen took her purse and instructed her to sit down on the sofa. Then, Carmen removed her mother's shoes and put her fluffy slippers on her sore feet. Finally, she brought her speechless mother a cup of piping hot tea.

"I already started dinner," said Carmen, "so you can rest for a while."

"Well, Carmen!" exclaimed her mother. "This is the most wonderful surprise I could ever have! Thank you so much!"

Carmen just smiled. It made her feel good to know that she had been the cause of her mother's happiness—and it had not been difficult at all!

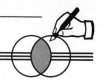

A Poem Can Tell a Story

Directions Read this poem. Think about the story it tells. Then, complete the blank story map on page 28.

The Children's Hour
by Henry Wadsworth Longfellow

Between the dark and the daylight,
    When the night is beginning to lower,
Comes a pause in the day's occupations,
    That is known as the Children's Hour.

I hear in the chamber above me
    The patter of little feet,
The sound of a door that is opened,
    And voices soft and sweet.

From my study I see in the lamplight,
    Descending the broad hall stair,
Grave Alice, and laughing Allegra,
    And Edith with golden hair.

A whisper, and then a silence:
    Yet I know by their merry eyes
They are plotting and planning together
    To take me by surprise.

A sudden rush from the stairway,
    A sudden raid from the hall!
By three doors left unguarded
    They enter my castle wall!

They climb up into my turret
    O'er the arms and back of my chair;
If I try to escape, they surround me;
    They seem to be everywhere.

They almost devour me with kisses,
    Their arms about me entwine,
Till I think of the Bishop of Bingen
    In his Mouse-Tower on the Rhine!

Do you think, o blue-eyed banditti,
    Because you have scaled the wall,
Such an old mustache as I am
    Is not a match for you all!

I have you fast in my fortress,
    And will not let you depart,
But put you down into the dungeon
    In the round-tower of my heart.

And there will I keep you forever,
    Yes, forever and a day,
Till the walls shall crumble to ruin,
    And moulder in dust away!

Name _____

Date _____

A=

B=

C=

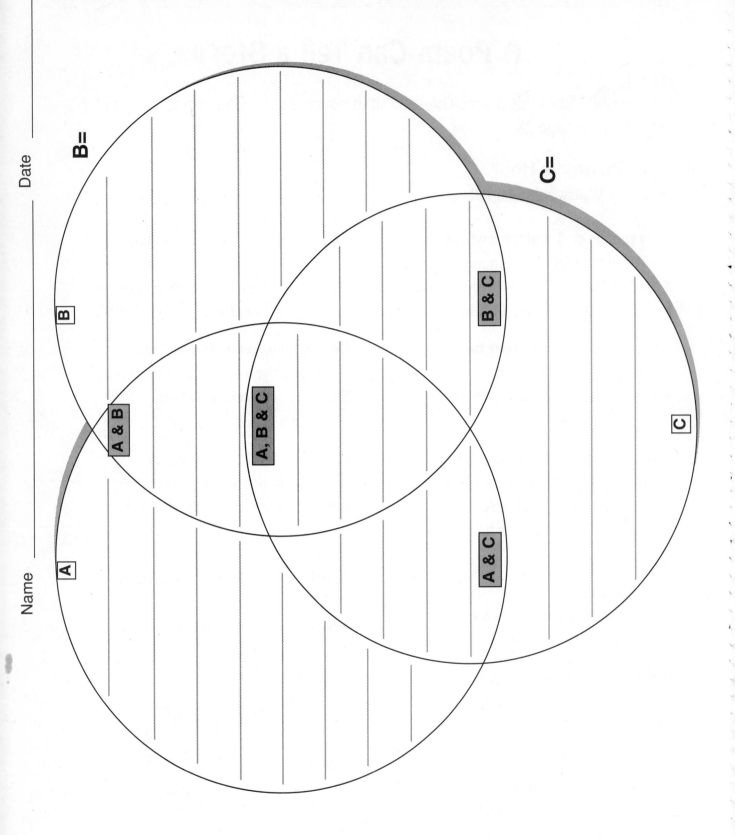

A

B

A & B

A, B & C

B & C

A & C

C

A= green

B= plant

C= food for people

B

tulip
red maple

cauliflower
carrot

B & C

A & B

tree leaves
poison ivy

A, B & C

lettuce
celery
broccoli

A

traffic light
emeralds
green crayon

green gelatin
green icepop

A & C

pasta
bread
steak

C

33

Where Does It Go?

A **Venn diagram** helps you to group things according to how they are alike or different.

Directions ➤ Use the blank Venn diagram on page 32. Follow the directions in 1–4. Then, use what you know to put each thing in the correct place on the diagram.

1. Write **in sky** next to A =.

2. Write **gives heat** next to B =.

3. Write **gives light** next to C =.

4. Think: Is it in the sky? Does it give off heat? Does it give off light? Write **yes** or **no**.

	in the sky?	gives off heat?	gives off light?
rain	_____	_____	_____
stove	_____	_____	_____
glow stick	_____	_____	_____
star	_____	_____	_____
fire	_____	_____	_____
radiator	_____	_____	_____
your body	_____	_____	_____
cloud	_____	_____	_____
light bulb	_____	_____	_____
Sun	_____	_____	_____
flashlight	_____	_____	_____
lightning	_____	_____	_____

5. Are there spaces that have no words in them? _____

What are they? _____

6. Can you think of anything that could go into these spaces? _____

7. Try to add one word to each of the other sections of the Venn diagram.

Word	Group	Characteristics	Definition

Use what you have learned from the chart to make a sentence for each word.

1. _____

2. _____

3. _____

4. _____

5. _____

Word	Group	Characteristics	Definition
vegetable	plant	grows in gardens, often crunchy, good to eat	any green, leafy plant of which part (seed, stem, fruit, or leaf) is used for food
cactus	plant	grows in desert, many sizes, needs little water	any desert plant with fleshy stem, spine-like leaves, and often showy flowers
flower	plant	can be wild or grow in garden, beautiful blooms	the seed-producing part of a plant, often with colorful blossoms
tree	plant	large plants, have leaves or needles, homes for animals	a woody plant with one main stem or trunk with many branches, usually quite tall
herb	plant	used as seasonings, leafy plants	green, leafy plants that are used as medicines and flavorings

Use what you have learned from the chart to make a sentence for each word.

1. Lettuce is a vegetable whose leaves are good to eat.

2. The cactus plants were painful to touch but beautiful to see.

3. I love to see the flowers of the orange trees.

4. My father planted a tree when he was young, and now it towers above his mother's house.

5. Fresh herbs add wonderful flavors to your cooking.

Something in Common

A **vocabulary grid** can help you to remember new words and their meanings.

Directions Use the words in one of these exercises to complete the blank vocabulary grid on page 35. Then, make a sentence for each word.

1. Group: Sciences
   geography
   astronomy
   geology
   biology
   oceanography

2. Group: Mathematical Terms
   parallel
   intersecting
   arc
   angle
   perpendicular

3. Group: Parts of the Earth
   atmosphere
   outer core
   inner core
   crust
   mantle

4. Group: Types of Art
   watercolor
   collage
   pastel
   tempera
   etching

Name _____ Date _____

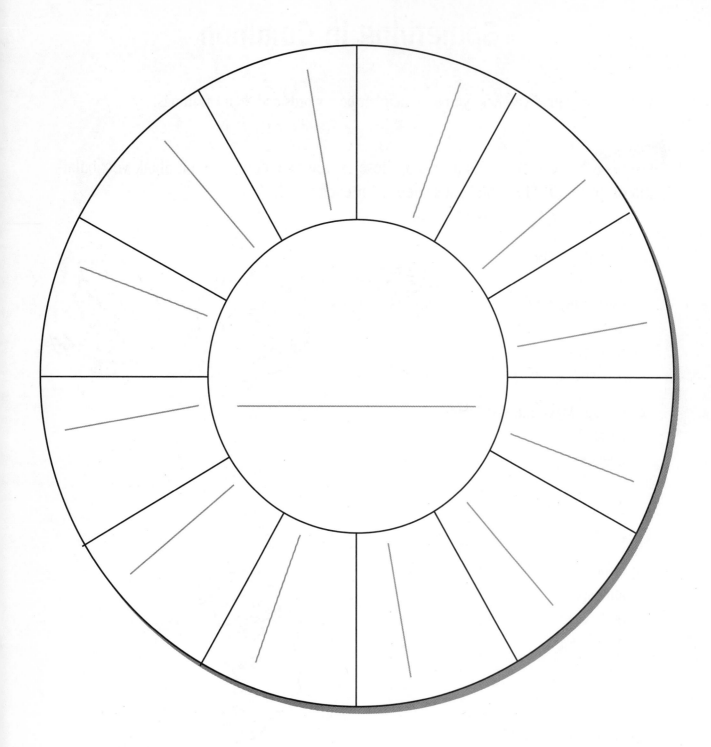

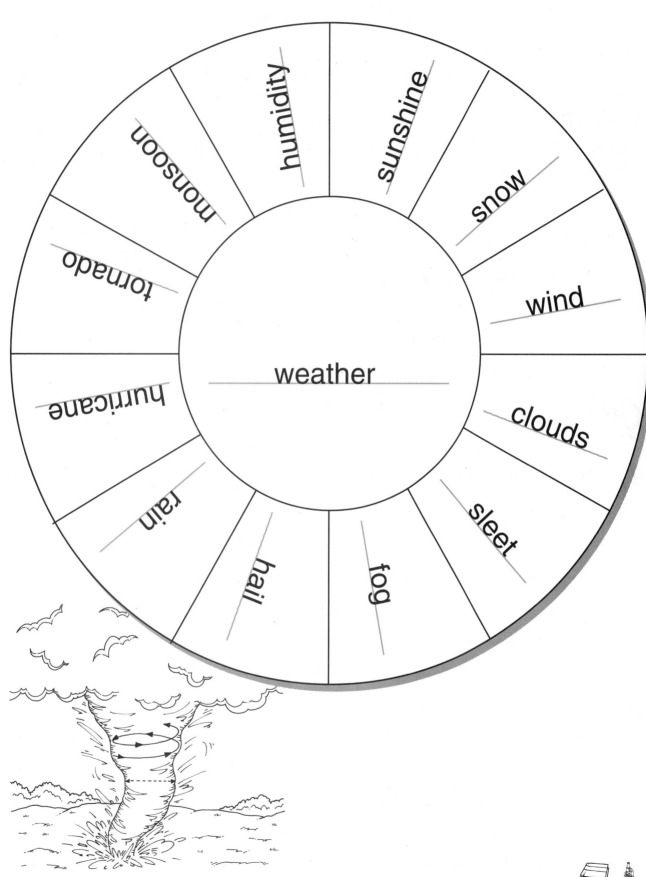

Word Wheel: weather — humidity, sunshine, snow, wind, clouds, sleet, fog, hail, rain, hurricane, tornado, monsoon

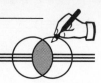

Free Wheeler

A **word wheel** helps you to expand your thinking. The center of the wheel shows your main idea. The "spokes" of the wheel show the words that you brainstorm from your main idea.

 Choose one of these activities. Use the blank word wheel on page 38 to complete the activity. Write the bold word that you chose in the center of the circle. Then, brainstorm to find words for the spokes of the word wheel.

Activity 1:
Brainstorm about your **favorite activities** or **sports**.

Activity 2:
Brainstorm about your **favorite school subject**.

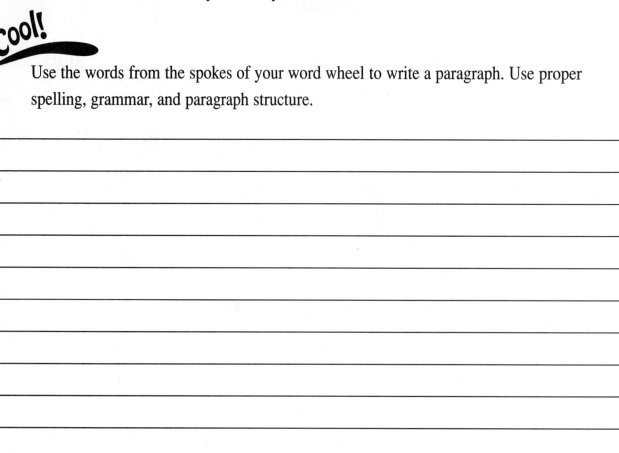

Activity 3:
Brainstorm about a **career** that you think you would like to have.

Cool!

Use the words from the spokes of your word wheel to write a paragraph. Use proper spelling, grammar, and paragraph structure.

_____

_____

_____

_____

_____

_____

_____

_____

_____

_____

_____

Name _____ Date _____

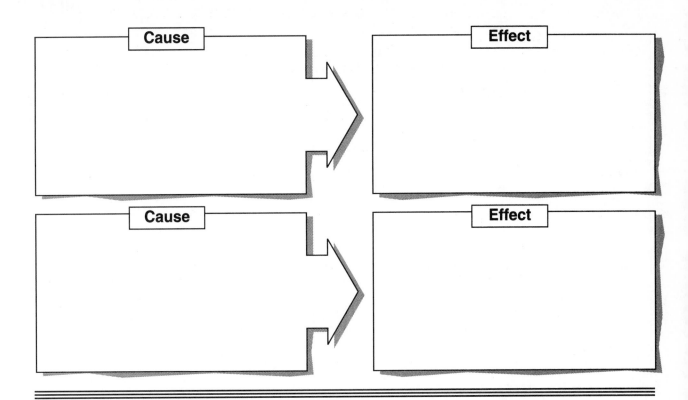

Cause

Effect

Cause

Effect

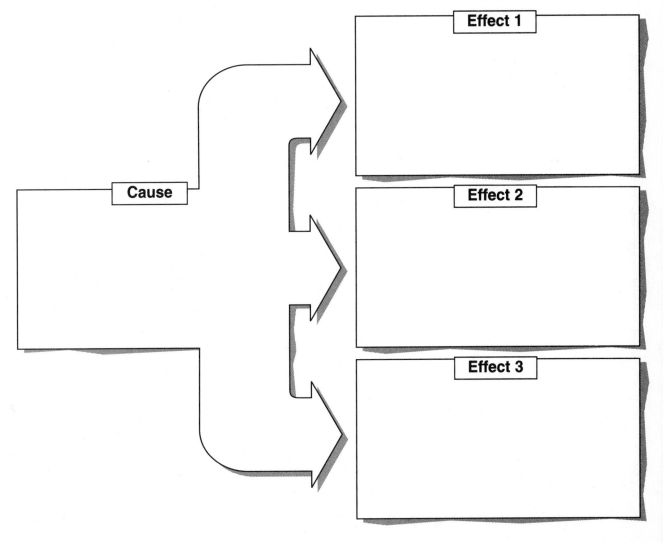

Effect 1

Cause

Effect 2

Effect 3

Cause		**Effect**
The ice melted off the mountains.	→	The rivers rose and flooded the streets.

Cause		**Effect**
Explorers were curious about their world.	→	They traveled and discovered new lands.

Effect 1

A land bridge formed between Asia and the Americas.

Cause

The first Ice Age ended.

Effect 2

Animals migrated to the Americas in search of food.

Effect 3

Hunters followed the animals and settled in the Americas.

Diagrams: Cause and Effect
Graphic Organizers Across the Curriculum 5, SV 3418-5

Ruth Law

Directions Read the story. Consider what causes things to happen in the story. Think about what the effects are. Look for cases where a cause had one effect. Look for a case where one cause had more than one effect. Then, complete the blank cause and effect diagrams on page 41. Use the one on the bottom for a cause that had more than one effect.

Throughout history, there have been many women who have become accomplished pilots. Women, however, were not encouraged in their pursuit of a pilot's license. It was not considered proper or even possible for a woman to fly a large plane! In spite of this, women did become pilots and fly planes. Several of them even broke aviation records.

One of these women was Ruth Law. In 1916, Ruth attempted to fly from Chicago to New York City in one day. She would set a record for uninterrupted flight across the country. Ruth encountered some difficulties as she prepared for her flight. She had tried to get a larger plane, but she was denied by the manufacturer. He did not believe a woman could handle a larger plane. The small plane had to be outfitted with a second gas tank, but to compensate for the extra weight of the gasoline, the lights were removed.

It was November when Ruth attempted her flight. Her plane did not protect her from the weather in any way. She dressed in many layers and put a skirt on over the rest of her clothes, as women were expected always to wear skirts in those days. She had to navigate with maps that were attached to her leg and with a compass.

Ruth was forced to land before she got to New York because she ran out of fuel. She landed safely, refueled, and started out again. It began to get dark, however, and without her lights, Ruth could not fly at night. She had to land two hours short of New York City. She had not made her goal, but she had set a record for non-stop flight—590 miles! She flew into New York City to great fanfare the next day.

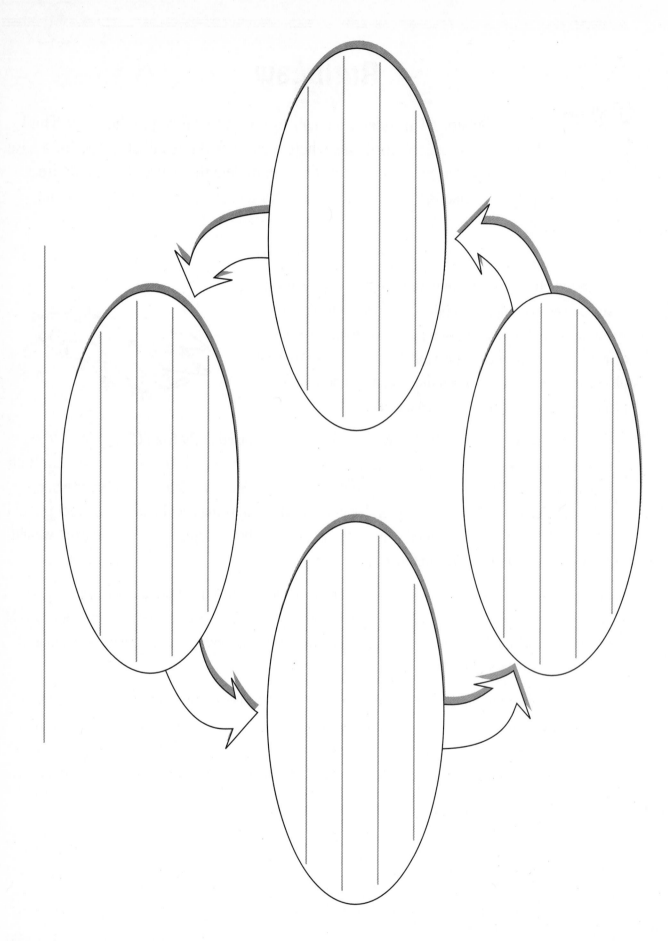

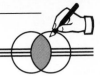

Ruth Law

Directions Read the story. Consider what causes things to happen in the story. Think about what the effects are. Look for cases where a cause had one effect. Look for a case where one cause had more than one effect. Then, complete the blank cause and effect diagrams on page 41. Use the one on the bottom for a cause that had more than one effect.

Throughout history, there have been many women who have become accomplished pilots. Women, however, were not encouraged in their pursuit of a pilot's license. It was not considered proper or even possible for a woman to fly a large plane! In spite of this, women did become pilots and fly planes. Several of them even broke aviation records.

One of these women was Ruth Law. In 1916, Ruth attempted to fly from Chicago to New York City in one day. She would set a record for uninterrupted flight across the country. Ruth encountered some difficulties as she prepared for her flight. She had tried to get a larger plane, but she was denied by the manufacturer. He did not believe a woman could handle a larger plane. The small plane had to be outfitted with a second gas tank, but to compensate for the extra weight of the gasoline, the lights were removed.

It was November when Ruth attempted her flight. Her plane did not protect her from the weather in any way. She dressed in many layers and put a skirt on over the rest of her clothes, as women were expected always to wear skirts in those days. She had to navigate with maps that were attached to her leg and with a compass.

Ruth was forced to land before she got to New York because she ran out of fuel. She landed safely, refueled, and started out again. It began to get dark, however, and without her lights, Ruth could not fly at night. She had to land two hours short of New York City. She had not made her goal, but she had set a record for non-stop flight—590 miles! She flew into New York City to great fanfare the next day.

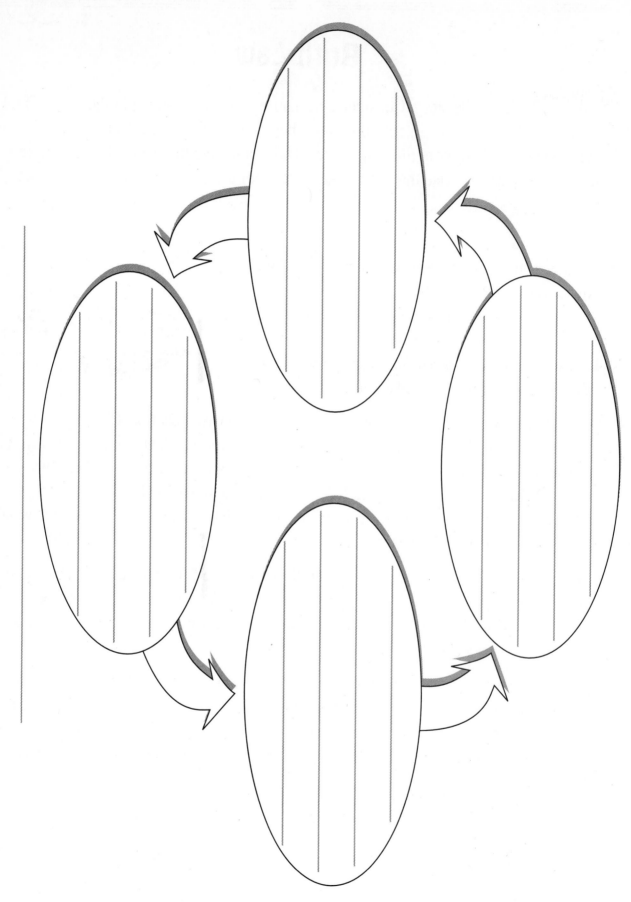

Diagrams: Cycle Diagram
Graphic Organizers Across the Curriculum 5, SV 3418-5

Blood Cycle

The heart pumps blood to the lungs where it picks up oxygen.

The blood leaves the organs and returns to the heart through veins.

The blood with oxygen goes to the heart.

The heart pumps the blood with oxygen through arteries into all of the organs of the body.

A Life Cycle

A **cycle diagram** shows how things change over time.

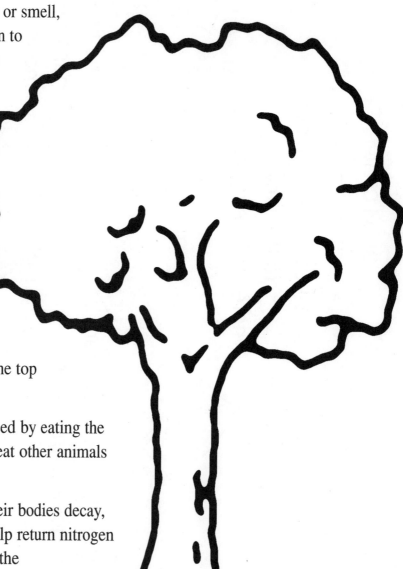

Directions   Read the information below about the nitrogen cycle. Then, complete the blank cycle diagram on page 44 to show the nitrogen cycle.

Nitrogen is a gas. It has no taste or smell, but every living thing needs nitrogen to survive. How do plants and animals get the nitrogen they need?

Nitrogen moves from the atmosphere into the ground when lightning strikes or when farmers spread fertilizers. Bacteria in the soil also turn nitrogen gas into nitrogen that plants can use.

Plants get the nitrogen from the soil through their roots. Most nitrogen is found in the topsoil, or the top layer of earth.

Animals get the nitrogen they need by eating the nitrogen-rich plants. Some animals eat other animals that have eaten the plants.

When plants and animals die, their bodies decay, or break down. Different bacteria help return nitrogen from decayed plants and animals to the soil and air. The cycle begins again.

Name _____ Date _____

Topic: _____

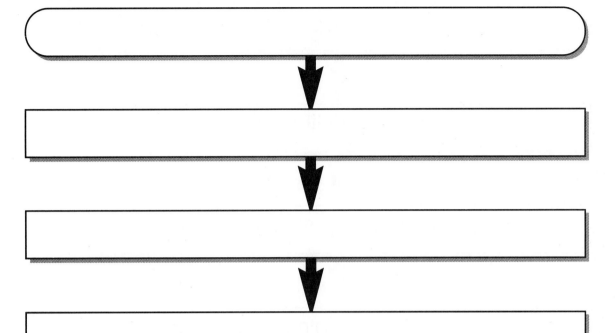

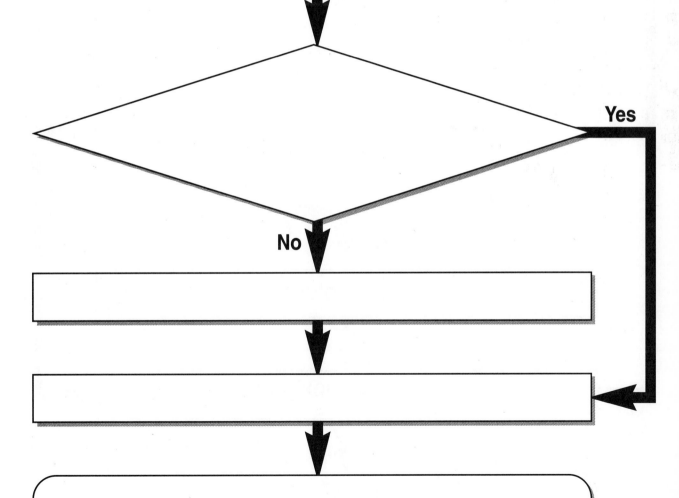

Topic: **Choosing Reference Books for a Report**

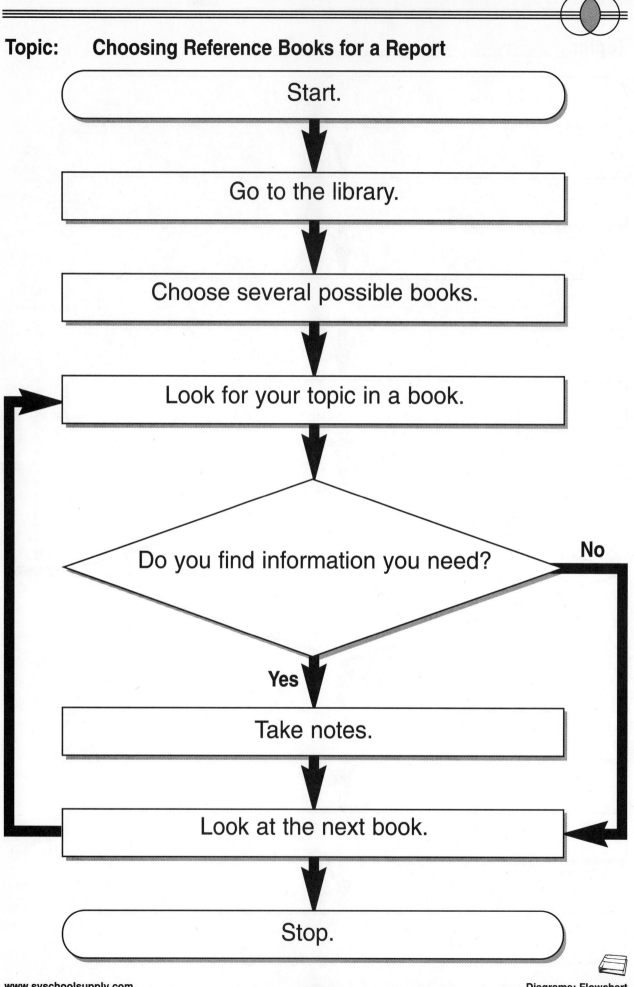

Start.

Go to the library.

Choose several possible books.

Look for your topic in a book.

Do you find information you need?

No

Yes

Take notes.

Look at the next book.

Stop.

Get Cooking

A **flowchart** helps to show the correct order of events in an action. Flowcharts are helpful in many different types of situations, from planning programs for computers to showing the right steps to take if someone is sick.

The parts of a flowchart have special shapes.

The **start** or **stop** box signals you.

The **instruction** box tells you what to do.

The **decision** box has a question that can be answered **yes** or **no**.

Directions ▶ Make a flowchart for baking cookies. Use the blank flowchart on page 47. Put the instructions in the correct order.

- Let cook a little longer.
- Put cookies in the oven.
- Mix cookies according to recipe.
- Put spoonfuls of dough on tray.
- Stop.
- Take cookies out of oven.
- Check cookies. Are they done?
- Start.

Cool!

Think of something that you could put into a flowchart. Make your own flowchart using the worksheet on page 47 as a guide. (You may add more instruction and decision boxes.)

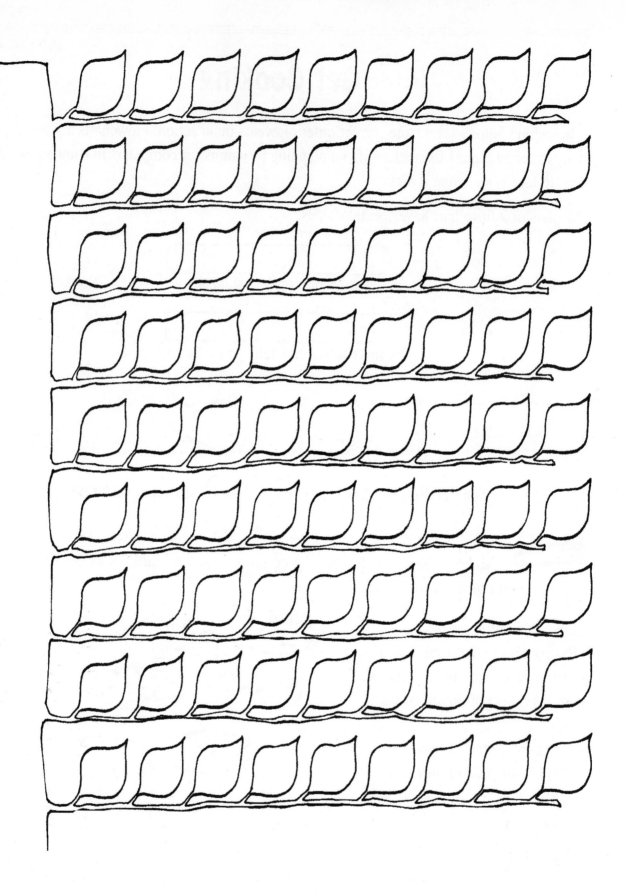

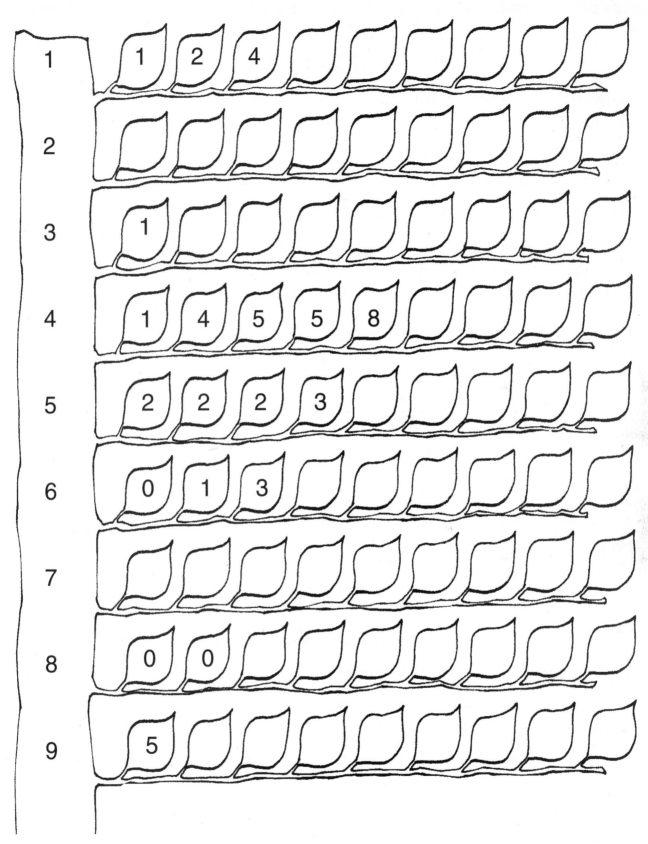

1	1	2	4							
2										
3	1									
4	1	4	5	5	8					
5	2	2	2	3						
6	0	1	3							
7										
8	0	0								
9	5									

Branch Out

Rasheed threw a baseball 20 times. He measured the number of feet that he threw the ball each time.

20 feet	64 feet	33 feet	35 feet	29 feet
52 feet	38 feet	32 feet	27 feet	23 feet
24 feet	58 feet	57 feet	27 feet	33 feet
55 feet	33 feet	46 feet	43 feet	40 feet

To organize the data in a **stem-and-leaf plot**, write the numbers in order from least to greatest. Group the data in rows according to the digit in the tens place.

Stem (Tens)	Leaves (Ones)
2	0 3 4 7 7 9
3	2 3 3 3 5 8
4	0 3 6
5	2 5 7 8
6	4

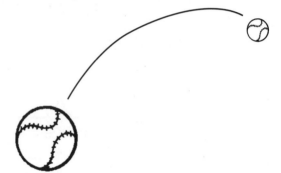

To find the lengths of the Rasheed's shortest and longest throws, look at the first and last numbers in the stem-and-leaf plot. His shortest throw was 20 feet. His longest throw was 64 feet.

Directions Answer questions 1–3 using the stem-and-leaf plot above.

1. How many of Rasheed's throws were shorter than 30 feet? _____

2. How many of Rasheed's throws were longer than 50 feet? _____

3. Which length occurs most often in the set? _____

4. Students recorded the scores they received on a spelling test. The scores were:
68, 68, 69, 69, 72, 73, 75, 75, 76, 84, 84, 86, 87, 88, 88, 88, 91, 92, 92, 93, 94, 95, 95, 98.
Show these scores on the blank stem-and-leaf plot on page 50.

Ask your teacher to fill a quart-size jar with marbles or jawbreakers. Have each student estimate the number of objects in the jar. Take the estimates and make a stem-and-leaf plot using the blank plot on page 50. Then, count the objects to see who is closest.

Name _____ Date _____

Details:

Main Idea:

Details:

Main Idea:

Details:

Scientists need no special suits for riding in a submersible.

The air pressure inside a submersible is the same as at the surface.

Main Idea:

Vehicles called submersibles help scientists explore deep parts of the ocean.

Some submersibles have mechanical hands for picking up objects on the ocean floor.

Scientists have seen things from inside a submersible that had never before been seen.

What's the Big Idea?

A good paragraph has a **main idea** that is supported by details. The main idea is presented in a topic sentence. All of the other sentences in the paragraph should relate to the topic sentence. If they don't, they don't belong in that paragraph.

Directions   Read this article about tricks that some animals play. Look for the main idea and the detail sentences. Write the main idea and four detail sentences in one of the blank graphic organizers on page 53.

Natural Tricks

Many animals protect themselves from predators by appearing to be something that they are not. Some moths look like hornets so that birds will leave them alone. One moth even has a fake stinger! Another moth appears to have giant eyes on its wings so it looks larger and more intimidating than it really is. One insect can make its hind end appear to be its head. When it jumps, it goes in the opposite direction from that which its predator expects. A certain spider will create fake, or decoy, spiders in its web to ward off danger. It builds the decoy spiders with masses of silk and pieces of dead insects. Predators will often attack the fake spiders instead of the real one.

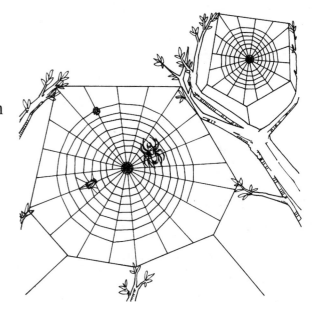

Directions   Find a paragraph in a book of your own choice. Find the main idea and detail sentences in the paragraph. Complete the second blank graphic organizer on page 53.

Information Source

Title _____

Author _____

Name of magazine or research book (encyclopedia, atlas, or other source)

_____

Page or pages where information was found _____

Notes _____

_____

_____

_____

_____

_____

_____

Information Source

Title _____

Author _____

Name of magazine or research book (encyclopedia, atlas, or other source)

_____

Page or pages where information was found _____

Notes _____

_____

_____

_____

_____

_____

_____

What's the Big Idea?

A good paragraph has a **main idea** that is supported by details. The main idea is presented in a topic sentence. All of the other sentences in the paragraph should relate to the topic sentence. If they don't, they don't belong in that paragraph.

Directions Read this article about tricks that some animals play. Look for the main idea and the detail sentences. Write the main idea and four detail sentences in one of the blank graphic organizers on page 53.

Natural Tricks

Many animals protect themselves from predators by appearing to be something that they are not. Some moths look like hornets so that birds will leave them alone. One moth even has a fake stinger! Another moth appears to have giant eyes on its wings so it looks larger and more intimidating than it really is. One insect can make its hind end appear to be its head. When it jumps, it goes in the opposite direction from that which its predator expects. A certain spider will create fake, or decoy, spiders in its web to ward off danger. It builds the decoy spiders with masses of silk and pieces of dead insects. Predators will often attack the fake spiders instead of the real one.

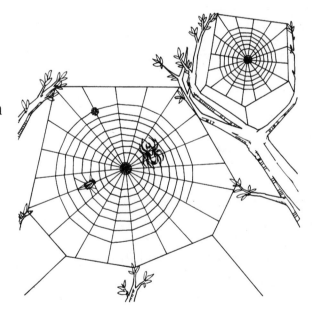

Directions Find a paragraph in a book of your own choice. Find the main idea and detail sentences in the paragraph. Complete the second blank graphic organizer on page 53.

Name _____ Date _____

Information Source

Title _____

Author _____

Name of magazine or research book (encyclopedia, atlas, or other source)

_____

Page or pages where information was found _____

Notes _____

_____

_____

_____

_____

_____

Information Source

Title _____

Author _____

Name of magazine or research book (encyclopedia, atlas, or other source)

_____

Page or pages where information was found _____

Notes _____

_____

_____

_____

_____

_____

What's the Big Idea?

A good paragraph has a **main idea** that is supported by details. The main idea is presented in a topic sentence. All of the other sentences in the paragraph should relate to the topic sentence. If they don't, they don't belong in that paragraph.

Directions Read this article about tricks that some animals play. Look for the main idea and the detail sentences. Write the main idea and four detail sentences in one of the blank graphic organizers on page 53.

Natural Tricks

Many animals protect themselves from predators by appearing to be something that they are not. Some moths look like hornets so that birds will leave them alone. One moth even has a fake stinger! Another moth appears to have giant eyes on its wings so it looks larger and more intimidating than it really is. One insect can make its hind end appear to be its head. When it jumps, it goes in the opposite direction from that which its predator expects. A certain spider will create fake, or decoy, spiders in its web to ward off danger. It builds the decoy spiders with masses of silk and pieces of dead insects. Predators will often attack the fake spiders instead of the real one.

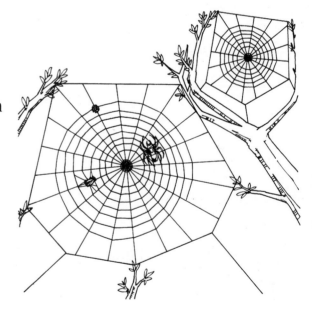

Directions Find a paragraph in a book of your own choice. Find the main idea and detail sentences in the paragraph. Complete the second blank graphic organizer on page 53.

Information Source

Title _____

Author _____

Name of magazine or research book (encyclopedia, atlas, or other source)

_____

Page or pages where information was found _____

Notes _____

_____

_____

_____

_____

_____

_____

Information Source

Title _____

Author _____

Name of magazine or research book (encyclopedia, atlas, or other source)

_____

Page or pages where information was found _____

Notes _____

_____

_____

_____

_____

_____

_____

Topic: Dakota (Sioux) Indians

Information Source

Title _____ Who Are the Sioux? _____

Author _____ Cameron Davis _____

Name of magazine or research book (encyclopedia, atlas, or other source)

_____ History Digest _____

Page or pages where information was found _____ pages 35-38 _____

Notes Lived in Minnesota and South Dakota. Real Name: Dakota Indians (Sioux means "little snake." Name given to them by enemies.) Hunted buffalo which they depended on for everything from food to shelter and clothing. Nomadic: means they moved a lot. Everything they had was easy to move and not easy to break (dishes made of hide instead of glass)

_____

Information Source

Title _____ North American Indians _____

Author _____ Susan Liptak _____

Name of magazine or research book (encyclopedia, atlas, or other source)

_____ N/A _____

Page or pages where information was found _____ pages 20, 23, 68 _____

Notes Clothes were very colorful. Lots of beadwork. Children taught by grandparents and parents. Ate wild fruits and vegetables. Gathered food in fall and stored it for winter. Marriage and family very important. Used every part of the buffalo (bones for knives, horns for cups and spoons)

_____

_____

_____

Take Note!

Note cards are an important part of writing a report. If you keep neat, organized note cards, writing will be easier and and your report will be better.

Directions ➤ Choose one of these topics. Find information on the subject in books or on the Internet. Use at least four sources to find information. Complete the blank note cards on page 56 with the information you find. (Save your completed note cards for another exercise.)

Topic 1: Toys in the 1800s

Find out what toys children played with 200 years ago.

Topic 2: Transportation in the 1800s

Find out how people got from place to place in the 1800s.

Topic 3: Clothing in the 1800s

Find out what people were wearing in the 1800s.

Name _____ Date _____

Topic: _____

I. _____

(Main Heading)

A. _____

(Subheading)

B. _____

(Subheading)

C. _____

(Subheading)

II. _____

(Main Heading)

A. _____

(Subheading)

B. _____

(Subheading)

C. _____

(Subheading)

III. _____

(Main Heading)

A. _____

(Subheading)

B. _____

(Subheading)

C. _____

(Subheading)

Topic: ___Lives of the Dakota Indians_____

I. _____Buffalo_____
(Main Heading)

   A. _____Followed the buffalo around the plains; never settled down_____
(Subheading)

   B. _____Used every part of the buffalo, from skin to bones and muscle_____
(Subheading)

   C. _____Made tepees, bowls, clothing, bags, and tools from the buffalo_____
(Subheading)

II. _____Clothing_____
(Main Heading)

   A. _____Dakota women were very good at beading and quillwork_____
(Subheading)

   B. _____Clothes were colorful and had beautiful handwork on them_____
(Subheading)

   C. _____Hair decorated with colorful beads and feathers_____
(Subheading)

III. _____Family_____
(Main Heading)

   A. _____Babies were center of attention_____
(Subheading)

   B. _____Parents taught children in the ways of the Dakotas_____
(Subheading)

   C. _____Families had to work together to survive_____
(Subheading)

Organize Your Thoughts

An **outline** is a way to organize your notes and thoughts so that you can write clear, meaningful paragraphs. Before you make an outline, you should have done research on your subject and created note cards.

Directions Read these paragraphs. Make a short outline using the information in the paragraphs and the blank outline on page 59.

The first Olympic games took place in Greece more than 2,000 years ago. They did not have many different sports; there was only one race in which people competed. Only men were allowed to compete in these games.

Today, the Olympic games are open to all kinds of athletes. For each event, the International Olympic Committee considers different cities all over the world. They choose one in which to hold the games. At each event, several thousand athletes take part in more than 20 different sports.

Today's Special Olympics are a separate event from the Olympic games. People with disabilities compete against each other in a variety of events. Here, people overcome physical and mental challenges to feel the excitement, joy, and pride of competing in the games and winning Olympic medals.

Cool!

Research a subject that interests you. On page 56, there are blank note cards on which you can take your notes. If you have already done the note-taking exercise, use the notes you have already taken to create an outline. Use the blank outline on page 59 as your guide.

Name _____

Date _____

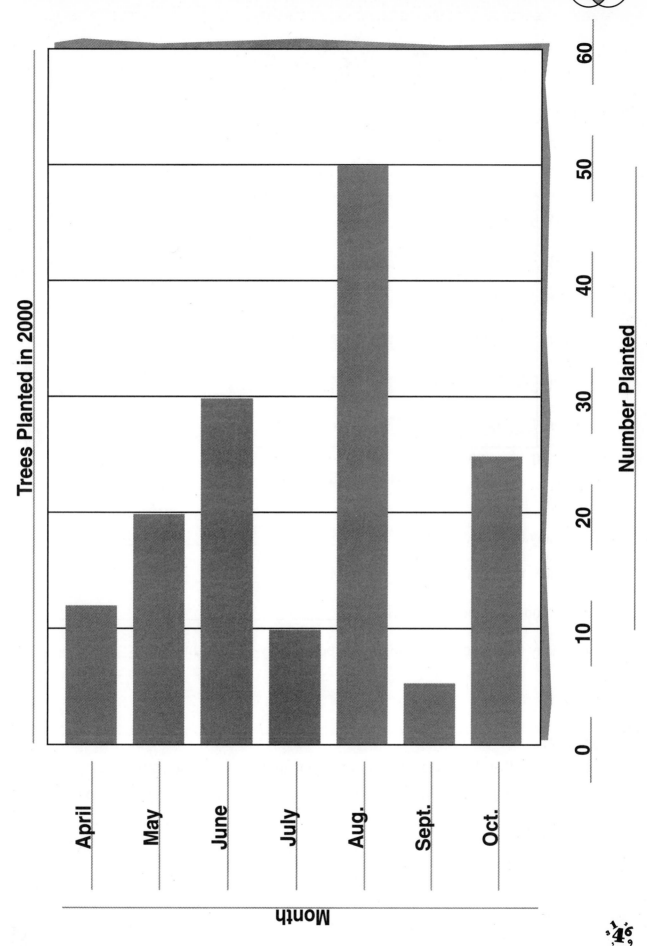

Trees Planted in 2000

Month: April, May, June, July, Aug., Sept., Oct.

Number Planted

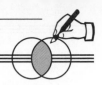

Trucks for Sale

Directions Use the bar graph for questions 1–4.

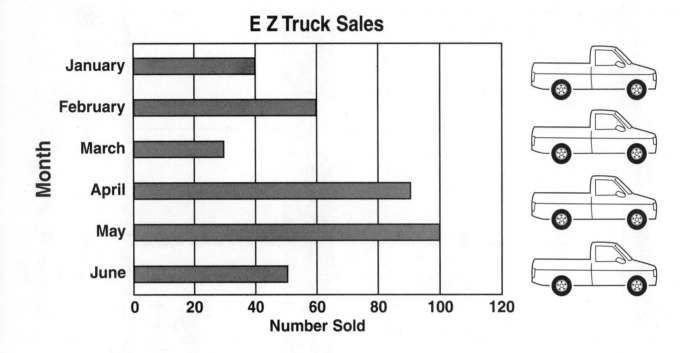

E Z Truck Sales

1. How many trucks were sold in June? _____

2. Were more trucks sold in January or in March? _____

3. Which month had the best sales? _____

4. How many trucks were sold altogether from January through June? _____

Cool!

Make a table that shows the number of students in your class who participate in various sports. Use the data from the table to make a bar graph using the blank graph on page 62. Choose a scale, write a title and labels for your graph, and then color in the bars.

Name

Date

65

Graphs: Double-Bar Graph
Graphic Organizers Across the Curriculum 5, SV 3418-5

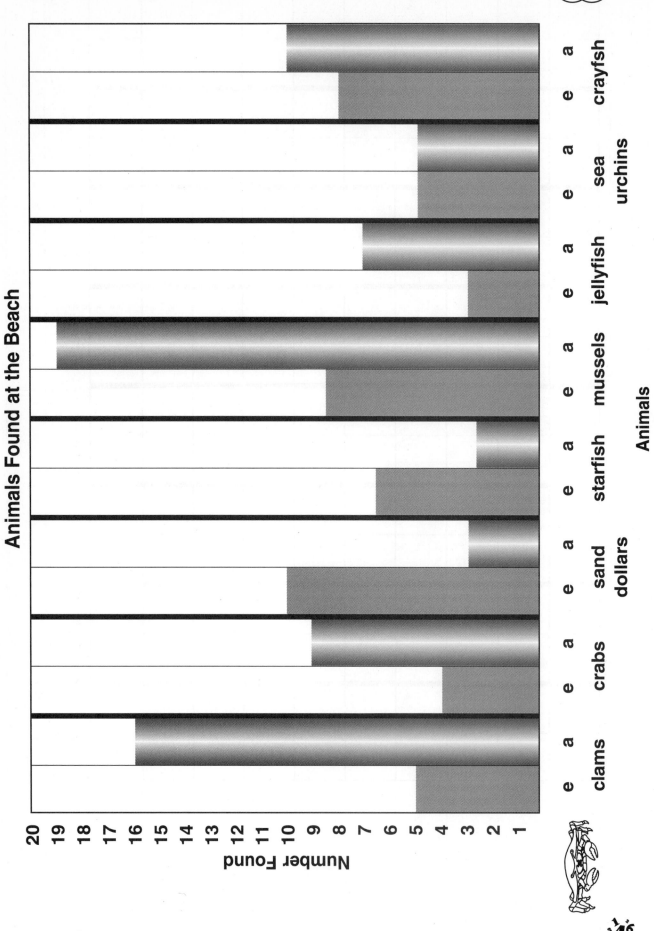

Animals Found at the Beach

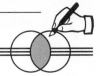

Estimate Weight

Directions For this exercise in estimating weight, you will need a balance scale and gram weights. Gather several items from your classroom that will fit on the scale. Estimate the weight of 8 items in grams, and fill in the bar graph with your estimates in the **e column**, using a colored pencil. Then, find the actual weight of each item, and enter that information on the graph in the **a column**, using a different colored pencil. How do your bars measure up?

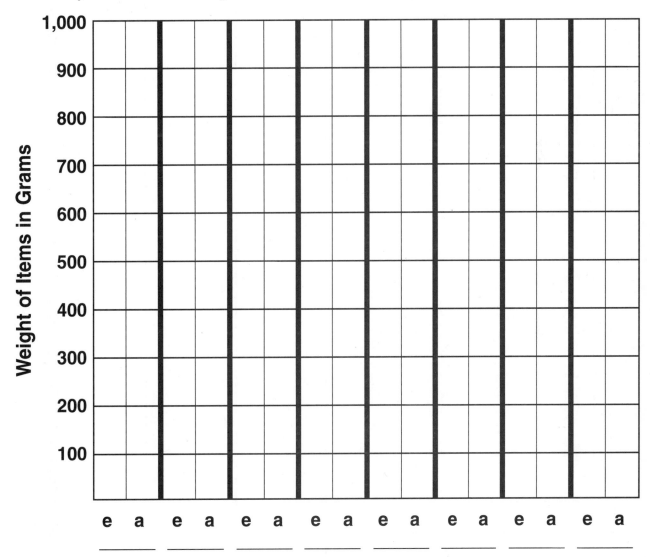

Weight of Items in Grams

1,000
900
800
700
600
500
400
300
200
100

e a e a e a e a e a e a e a e a

Item Weighed

If possible, take your work outside! Gather items from around your school to estimate and weigh. Use the blank graph on page 65 to chart your results.

Name _____

Date _____

Reasearch Papers Written by Each Class

Number of Papers

Class	Number of Papers
Mrs. Segi	🗎🗎🗎🗎
Mrs. Haji	🗎🗎🗎🗎🗎🗎🗎
Mr. Franco	🗎🗎🗎🗎🗎
Ms. Cappel	🗎🗎🗎🗎
Mr. Dunn	🗎🗎🗎

Each 🗎 = 5 papers

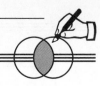

Get the Picture?

Directions Use the pictograph to answer questions 1–4.

Result of Student Council Election

Person	Number of Votes
Fran	☐ ☐ ☐ ☐ ☐ ☐ ☐ ☐ ⧖
Ben	☐ ☐ ☐ ☐ ☐ ☐
Crissy	☐ ☐ ☐ ☐ ☐ ☐ ☐ ☐ ☐ ☐
Anil	☐ ☐ ☐ ☐ ☐ ☐ ☐
Angelina	☐ ☐ ☐ ☐ ⧖

☐ = **10 votes**

1. Which 2 students got the same number of votes? _____

2. Who won the election? _____

3. How many votes did Fran get? _____

4. What was the total number of votes for all the students? _____

5. Who got the least number of votes? _____

Cool!

Take a survey to see how many pets each student in your class has. Organize your information by pets. Use the blank pictograph on page 68 to graph your results.

Name _____ Date _____

Graphs: Line Graph
Graphic Organizers Across the Curriculum 5, SV 3418-5

Title: Temperatures in Redwood for 1 week   **Key: My estimate** — · —
                                                         Actual temp. ———

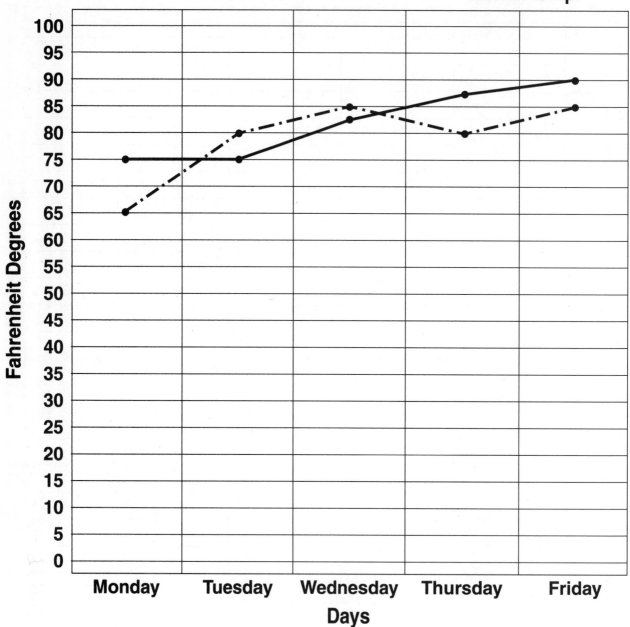

Name _____ Date _____

Weather Watch

Directions Keep track of the temperature in your town for 1 week. At the same time each day, guess what you believe the outside temperature is. Check a thermometer to see what the temperature actually is. Then, listen to the radio to hear what your local meteorologist says the temperature is.

Using 3 different colors, plot a 3-line graph showing your estimates, your thermometer readings, and the meteorologist's report for the week. Include a color key and a title. Are your lines close?

Title: _____ **Key:** _____

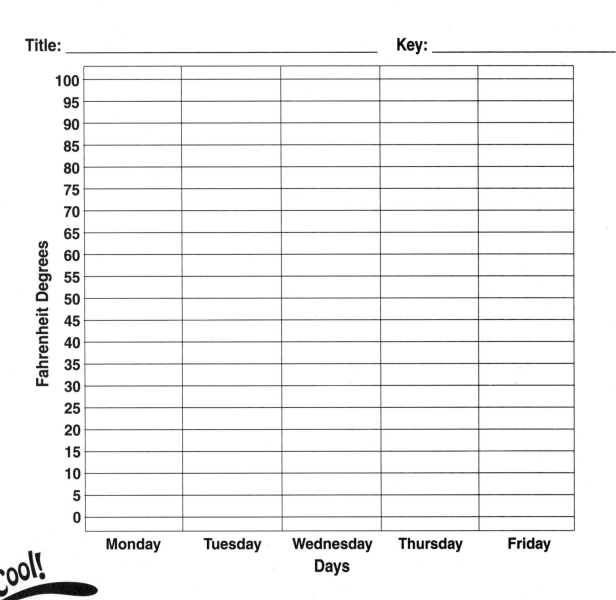

Cool!

Use the blank graph on page 71 to make a double-line graph. Follow the weather in another state. This time, you will have a line for your estimates and a line for the actual temperature for the day.

Name _____ Date _____

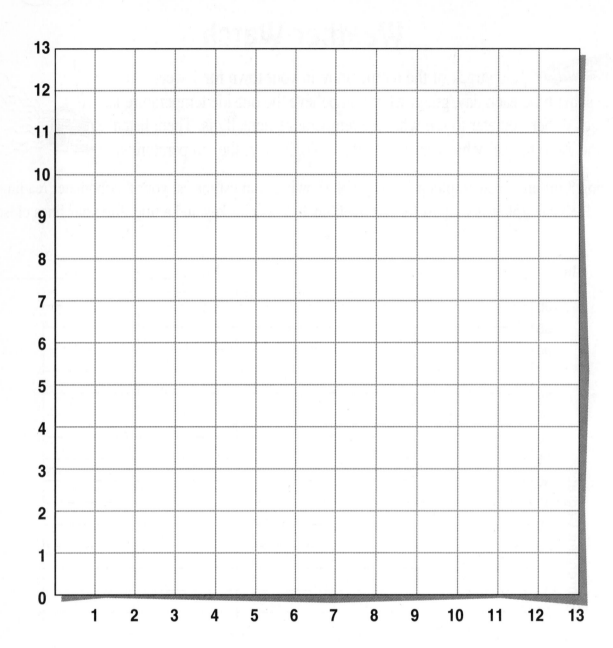

Graphs: Coordinate Graph

Graphic Organizers Across the Curriculum 5, SV 3418-5

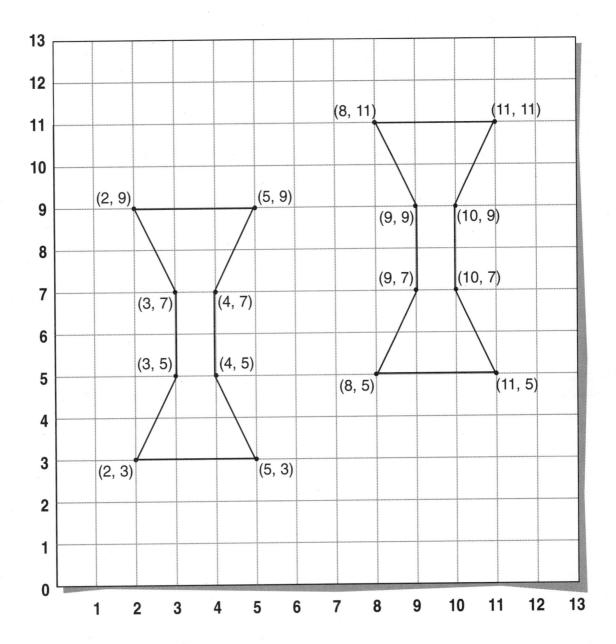

Transformations on a Coordinate Grid

When you move a figure, it is called a transformation. A translation is one type of transformation. When you translate, or slide, a figure on a coordinate grid, the coordinates change. The figure may move up or down, left or right, or both. Here is one example of translation.

3 spaces to the right

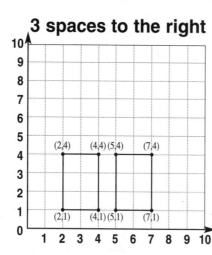

New ordered pairs:

(2,1) to (5,1)

(4,1) to (7,1)

(2,4) to (5,4)

(4,4) to (7,4)

Directions Translate each figure. Draw the new figure with its coordinates. Name the new ordered pairs.

1. Translate the figure 5 spaces to the right and 4 spaces up.

2. Translate the figure 3 spaces to the right and 4 spaces down.

3. Translate the figure 4 spaces to the left and 4 spaces down.

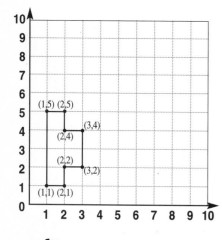

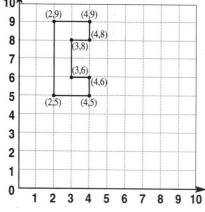

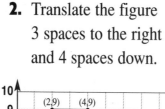

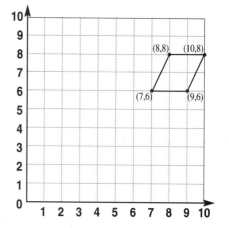

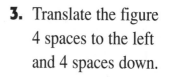

Cool!

Use the blank graph on page 74 to create your own translation. Make any figure you would like. Name the coordinate pairs, and tell what the translation is (for example, 2 spaces to the left, and 1 space down).

Name _____ Date _____

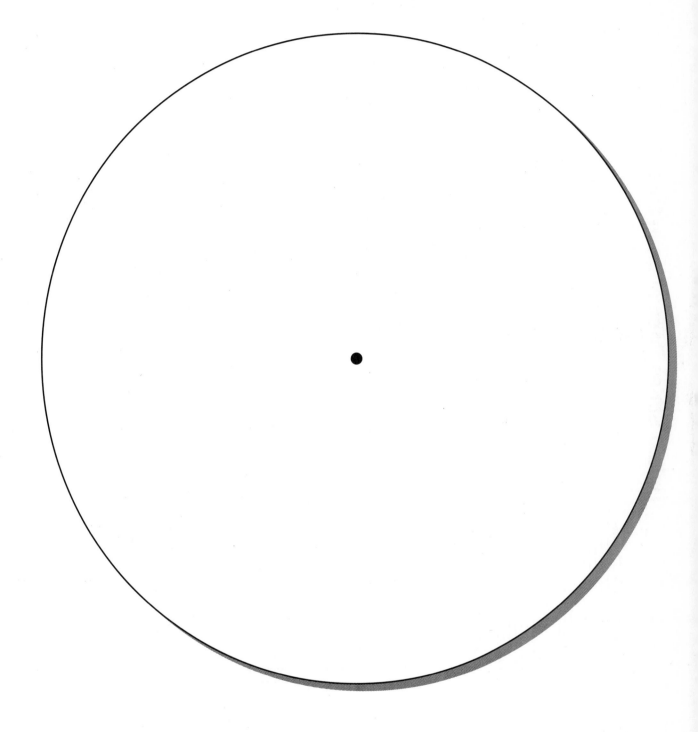

United States Population in 2050

Key	Nationality	%	Total Population
	Anglo American	52	202,000,000
	Hispanic American	21	81,000,000
	African American	16	62,000,000
	Asian American	10	41,000,000
	Native American	1	5,000,000

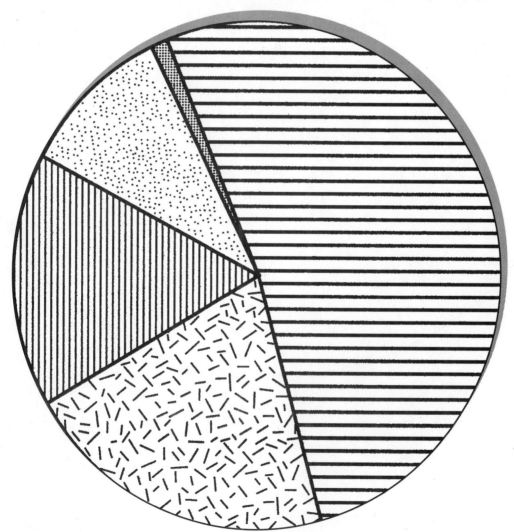

www.svschoolsupply.com
© Steck-Vaughn Company

Graphs: Pie Graph
Graphic Organizers Across the Curriculum 5, SV 3418-5

Zoo Graphs

 Directions Use the pie graphs to solve.

1. How many reptiles and amphibians are there at the zoo? _____

   _____

2. Of the herd animals at the zoo, 36 are gazelles. How many of the herd animals are not gazelles? _____
   How many more herd animals are there than reptiles and amphibians?_____

3. There are 28 birds in the endangered species section at the zoo. What percent is this? _____
   Write the percent on the graph.

4. What is the percent of reptiles at the zoo? _____
   Write the percent on the graph.
   How many reptiles are there? _____

5. Use the following information and the blank pie graph on page 77 to show the different types of predators at the zoo. Write the percentage and the number of each type of predator on the graph.

   There are 210 predators at the zoo.
      30% are small predators.
      10% are birds.
      20% are wolves and coyotes.
      40% are cats.

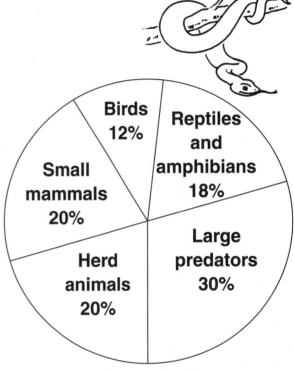

ANIMALS AT THE COLORADO CANYON INSTITUTE
(700 animals in all)

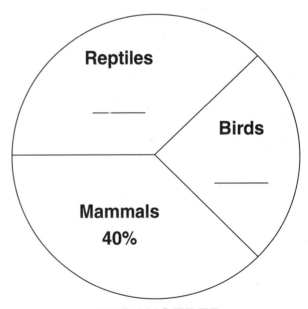

ENDANGERED SPECIES
(140 animals in all)

Graphs: Using and Making a Pie Graph
Graphic Organizers Across the Curriculum 5, SV 3418-5

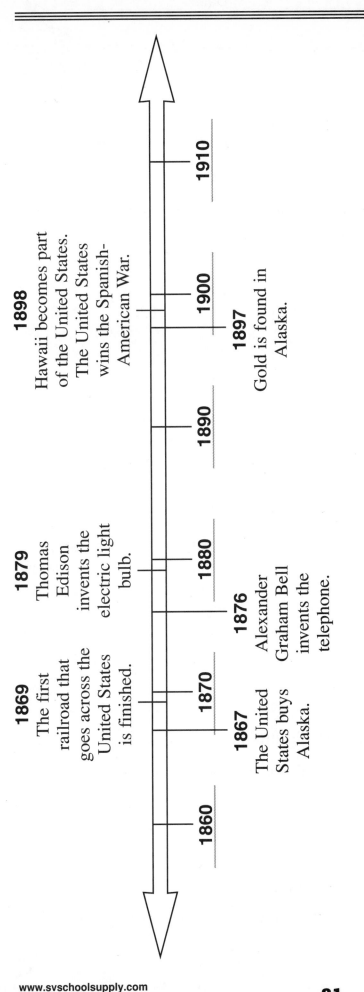

1910

1898
Hawaii becomes part of the United States. The United States wins the Spanish-American War.

1900

1897
Gold is found in Alaska.

1890

1879
Thomas Edison invents the electric light bulb.

1880

1876
Alexander Graham Bell invents the telephone.

1869
The first railroad that goes across the United States is finished.

1870

1867
The United States buys Alaska.

1860

1900 Hawaii becomes part of the U.S. The U.S. wins the Spanish-American War.

1898

1897 Gold is found in Alaska.

1890

1880

1879—invents the light bulb.

Thomas Edison

1876—— Alexander Graham Bell invents the telephone.

First railroad that goes across the U.S.

1870

1869——is finished.

1867—The U.S. buys Alaska.

1860

A Time for Change

The Patriots fought the British in the American Revolution from 1776 to 1783. During that time, each side won and lost several battles.

Directions ➤ Use the time line below to help you organize some of the important events that took place during the American Revolution.

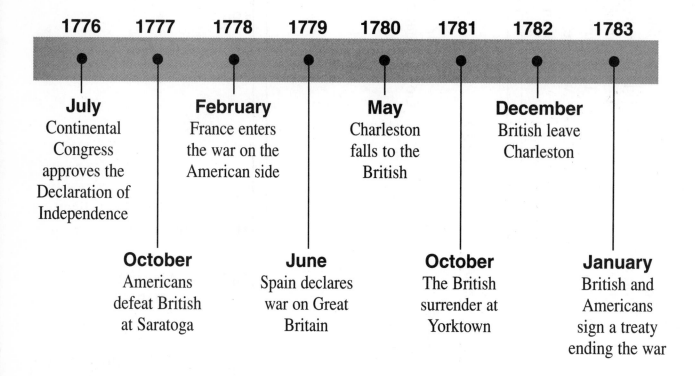

1776 1777 1778 1779 1780 1781 1782 1783

July
Continental Congress approves the Declaration of Independence

February
France enters the war on the American side

May
Charleston falls to the British

December
British leave Charleston

October
Americans defeat British at Saratoga

June
Spain declares war on Great Britain

October
The British surrender at Yorktown

January
British and Americans sign a treaty ending the war

1. What years does this time line span? _____

2. In what month and year did Charleston fall to the British? _____

3. How many years passed between the time the Continental Congress approved the

   Declaration of Independence and when the war ended? _____

Cool!

Look into the history of your state. Find several key dates on which important things happened for your state. Use a blank time line on page 80 to make a time line showing these dates and the events.

a.

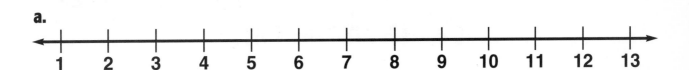

b.

c.

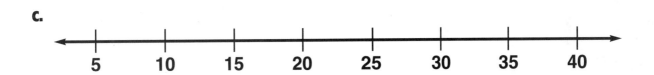

d.

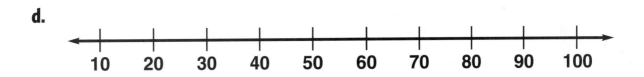

e.

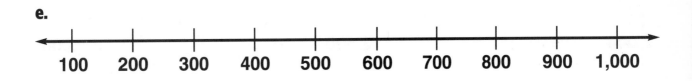

f.

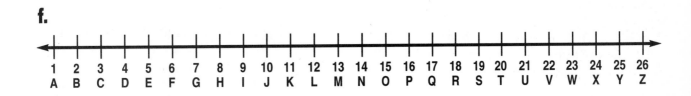

Lay It on the Line

You can use **number lines** to round whole numbers.
Round 3,467 to the nearest thousand.

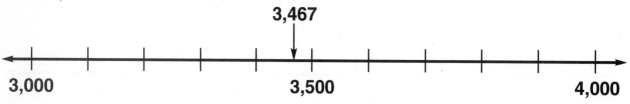

3,467

3,000   3,500   4,000

The number 3,467 is closer to 3,000 than to 4,000.
So, 3,467 rounded to the nearest thousand is 3,000.

Directions ▸ Mark the point where the number belongs on the number line. Round to the place of the underlined digit.

1. <u>5</u>67 rounds to: _____

500   550   600

2. 1,4<u>5</u>6 rounds to: _____

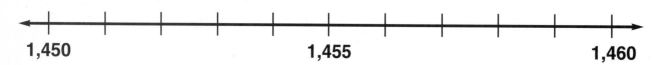

1,450   1,455   1,460

3. <u>3</u>,353 rounds to: _____

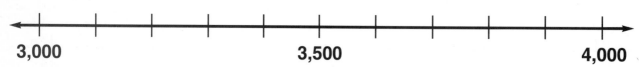

3,000   3,500   4,000

Cool!

Use number line **e** from page 83 to write some rounding problems. Trade papers with a classmate to solve.

NORTH AMERICA

Famous Explorers

Some famous explorers who visited North America have places named after them. Look at the map shown here to find out about some explorers who have had places named after them.

Directions ▶ Use the map to answer the questions.

1. What two places are named after the explorer Henry Hudson?

   _____

   _____

2. In 1616, William Baffin, an English explorer, traveled through part of what is now Canada. Circle the two places named after him.

3. What place is named after Hernando Cortés?

   _____

4. Which place is named after Christopher Columbus?

   _____

Cool!

Look at the blank map of North America on page 85. Locate, as closely as you can, where you are now. Mark on page 85 three of the places shown on the map above. Use the map scale on page 85 to estimate how far you are from each place.

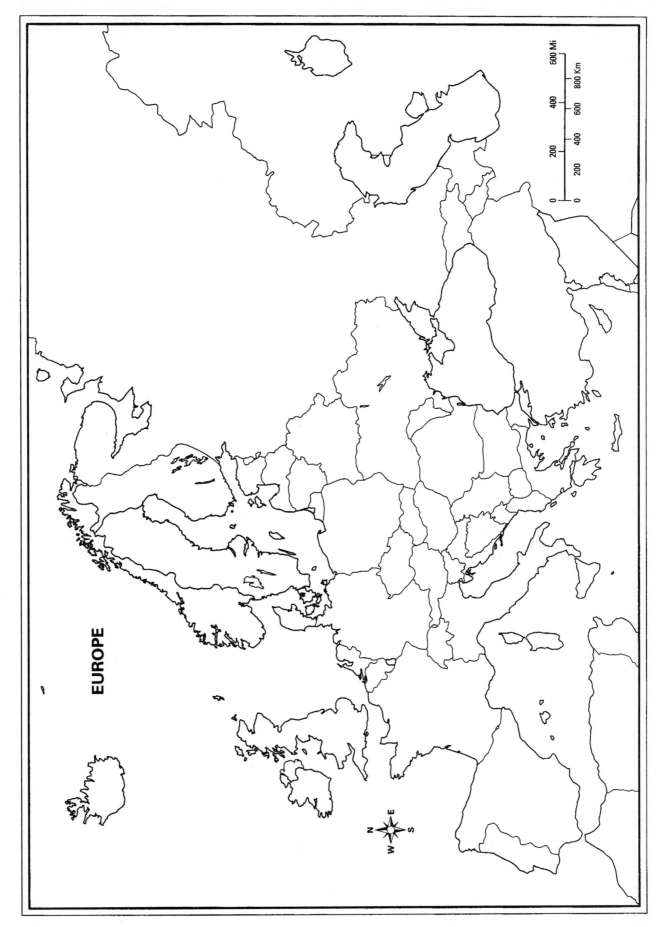

EUROPE

Name _____ Date _____

THE WORLD

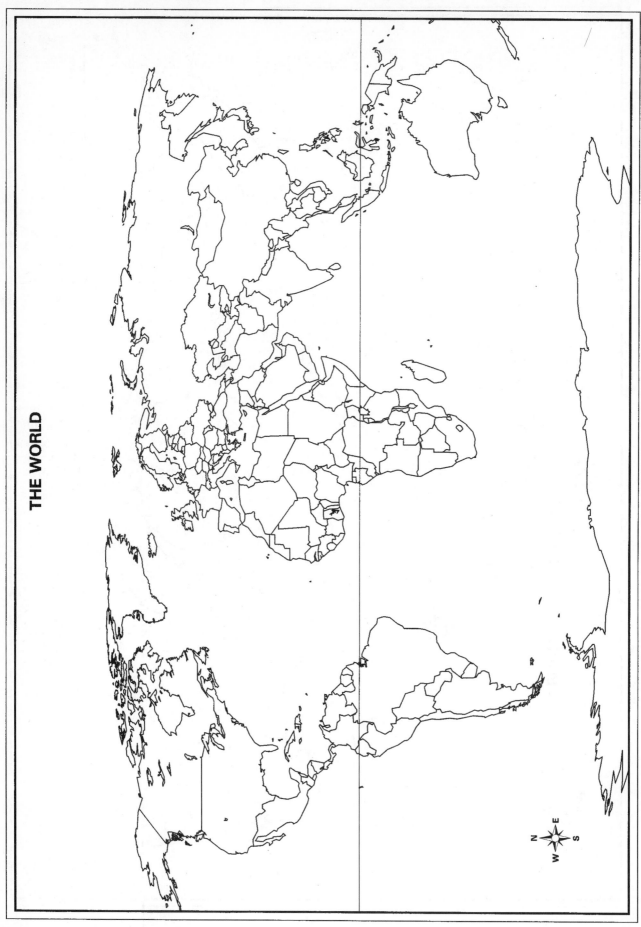

Food for Thought

The ancestors of the American Indians got their food in different ways. The places where they settled had a lot to do with the kind of food they ate.

Directions ▶ Look at the map below to answer the questions that follow.

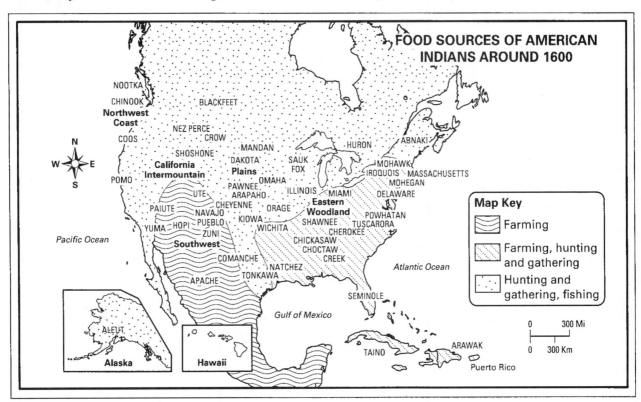

FOOD SOURCES OF AMERICAN INDIANS AROUND 1600

Map Key
- Farming
- Farming, hunting and gathering
- Hunting and gathering, fishing

1. Look at the map key. In what part of America did people get most of their food by farming?

_____

2. Which American Indian groups lived on the Northwest Coast?

_____

How did they get their food?

_____

3. How did the Seminole people get their food?

_____

Cool!

Look at the blank map of the world on page 88. How many of the world's seven continents can you label without help? Label all of the continents. You may use reference books to help you.

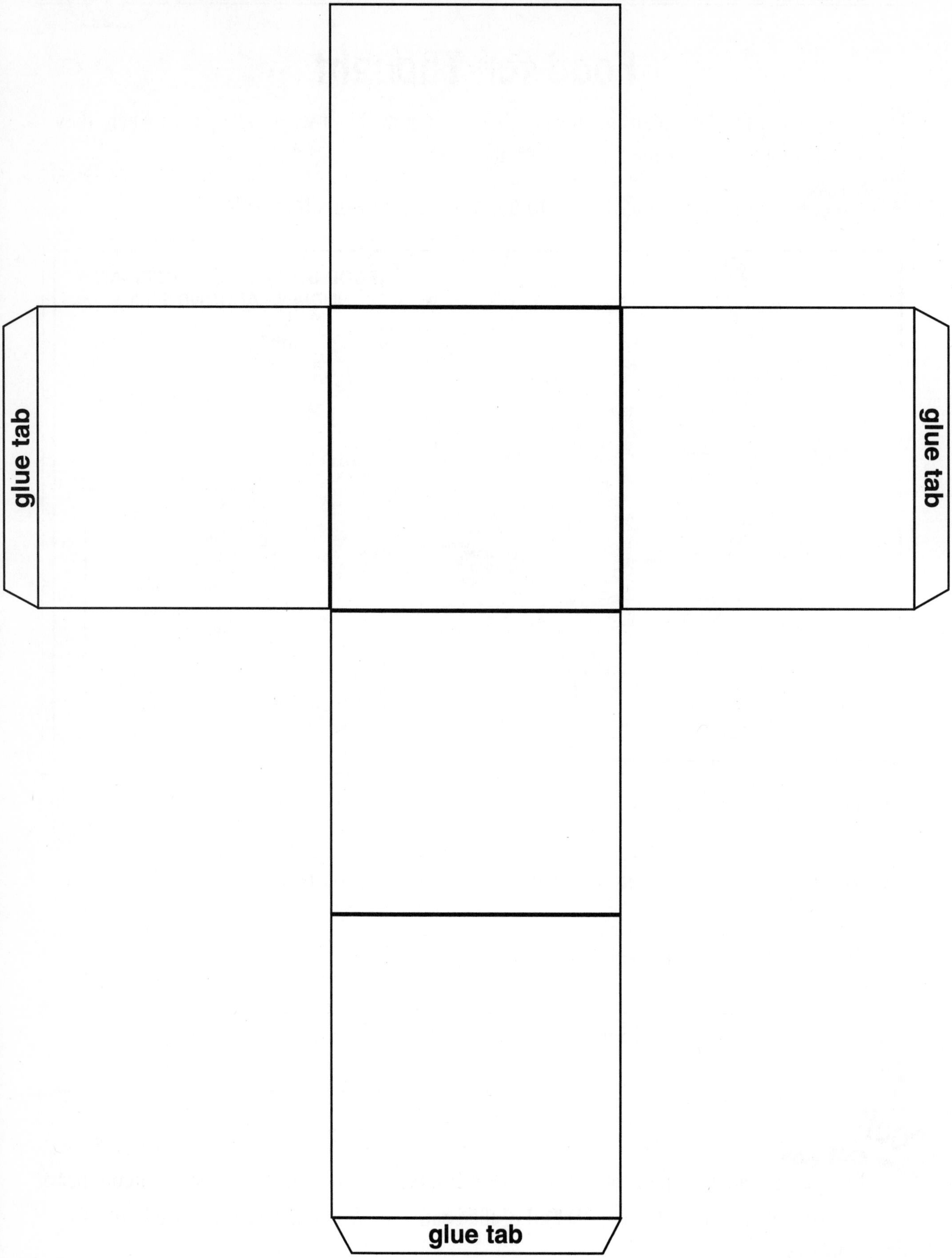

glue tab

glue tab

glue tab

www.svschoolsupply.com
© Steck-Vaughn Company

Cube It!

A **cube** can help you to think and write. You can write your ideas about something on each side of the cube. Then, cut out the cube and paste or tape it together. Toss the cube into the air. When it lands, write about the idea that faces up on the cube.

Directions Choose one of these activities. Use the blank cube on page 90 to complete the activity.

Activity 1:

Think about the way people did things hundreds of years ago. For example, how did they travel? Where did they get their food? On each side of the cube, write one thing that you think has changed. Make and toss your cube. Read the side that faces up. Talk about it. Find out more about it. Then, write about it.

Activity 2:

Think about the different kinds of places where animals can live. They may live where it is cold, or they may live in humid rain forests. On each side of the cube, name a kind of place. Make and toss your cube. Read the side that faces up. What kinds of animals live there? Find out. Write about them.

Activity 3:

There are many different types of writing. On your cube, write **news article**, **mystery**, **poetry**, **science fiction**, **historical fiction**, and **humorous**. Make and toss your cube. Read the side that faces up. Write something in that style. You may want to read some samples of that kind of writing before you begin.

WHAT IS THE WORD?
Write the word here.

_____

WHAT DOES THE WORD MEAN?
Write the meaning here.

_____

_____

_____

_____

_____

WHAT DOES THE WORD STAND FOR?
Draw a picture of it here.

HOW CAN YOU USE THE WORD?
Write a sentence using the word here.

_____

_____

_____

_____

_____

WHAT IS THE WORD?

Write the word here.

_____sextant_____

WHAT DOES THE WORD MEAN?

Write the meaning here.

An instrument used by navigators to find a ship's position. It measures the distance from the horizon to a star or the Sun.

WHAT DOES THE WORD STAND FOR?

Draw a picture of it here.

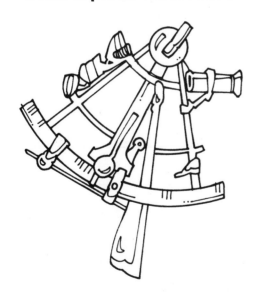

HOW CAN YOU USE THE WORD?

Write a sentence using the word here.

By using his sextant to find our position, the ship's navigator could tell that we were 400 miles from the nearest land.

Give It Meaning

Word cards can help you learn and remember new words. On the word cards, first write the word. Then, find the meaning of the word and write it on the next card. The third card is a place to illustrate what the word means. On the fourth card, use the word in a sentence.

Directions ➤ Get a new book from the school library or your town library. Follow these steps:

• As you read the book, write down any word that you do not know the meaning of. Keep a list of the words below.

• As you go along, complete word cards for the new words. Use the blank word cards on page 92.

• Each time you complete a set of word cards, re-read the sentence in which you first found the word.

• When you finish your book, you will have added new words to your vocabulary—and you will understand your reading better!

_____   _____

_____   _____

_____   _____

_____   _____

_____   _____

_____   _____

_____   _____

_____   _____

Graphic Organizers Across the Curriculum
Grade Five

Answer Key

P. 9
Answers will vary.

P. 12
1. the citizens
2. city manager
3. neighborhood services
4. technology

Family organizational charts will vary.

P. 15
1. migrate
2. camouflage
3. bear
4. whale, Canada goose, monarch butterfly
5. By blending with the environment, an animal can hide from predators.

Compare and contrast matrices will vary.

P. 18

	Swimming	Softball	Basketball	Track
Donna	Yes	X	X	X
Li	X	X	Yes	X
Sari	X	Yes	X	X
Evita	X	X	X	Yes

	Bermuda	California	Canada	New York City
Mari	X	X	Yes	X
Kiran	Yes	X	X	X
Bryan	X	X	X	Yes
Kim	X	Yes	X	X

P. 21
1. 243
2. 108
3. 21
4. 21
5. 15
6. 9
7. 540
8. 324
9. 72
10. 81
11. 24
12. 12

P. 24
1. the flight to New York
2. 1:34 P.M.
3. St. Louis, 2 hours and 35 minutes
4. 2:16 P.M.
5. Chicago

Schedules will vary.

P. 27
Check students' word webs.
1. Inventors
2. Athletes
3. Civil Rights Activists
4. Explorers

Paragraphs should contain accurate information from word web.

P. 30
Characters: Carmen and her mother
Setting: Carmen's house
Problem: Carmen's mother works hard; Carmen doesn't appreciate what her mother does.
Events: Carmen thinks she helps out a lot, but then she realizes she can do much more to help her mother out.
Solution: Carmen decides to do more to help her mother, who appreciates Carmen's new attitude.

P. 31
Characters: a father and his three daughters
Setting: the father's study
Problem: the girls want to surprise their father
Events: A father sits in his study and hears his girls sneaking down the stairs. They run in to surprise him.
Solution: The father is pleased to see his daughters and says he will keep them in his heart forever.

P. 34
Rain: yes, no, no
Stove: no, yes, yes
Glow stick: no, no, yes
Star: yes, yes, yes
Fire: no, yes, yes
Radiator: no, yes, no
Your body: no, yes, no
Cloud: yes, no, no
Light bulb: no, yes, yes
Sun: yes, yes, yes
Flashlight: no, yes, yes
Lightning: yes, yes, yes
In A: rain, cloud
In B: your body, radiator
In C: glow stick
In A&B: None
In A&C: None
In B&C: stove, fire, light bulb, flashlight
In A, B, & C: star, sun, lightning
5. Yes. A & B and A & C
6. Answers may vary; there may not be an answer.
7. Answers will vary.

P. 37
Answers will vary.
Definitions:
Sciences:
geography: study of Earth's surface, its division into continents, the climates, and animals and people that live in each place
astronomy: study of the universe, its stars, planets, etc., and their origins and compositions
geology: study of the history and structure of the Earth, rocks, fossils, etc.
biology: study of the origins, characteristics, life, and habits of plants and animals
oceanography: study of the ocean
Mathematical Terms:
parallel: extending in the same direction and being the same distance apart at every point so as to never meet
intersecting: crossing each other
arc: any part of a curve
angle: shape made by two planes intersecting, or where two lines meet at a common point
perpendicular: at right angles
Parts of the Earth:
atmosphere: the gases that surround the Earth
outer core: a liquid iron that surrounds the inner core
inner core: the center of the Earth
crust: the solid outer part of the Earth
mantle: a layer of the Earth between the crust and the core
Types of Art:
watercolor: a pigment or coloring-matter that is mixed with water to use as paint; a painting made with this paint
collage: a picture made from bits of objects pasted together on a surface
pastel: a ground coloring-matter, mixed with gum and formed into a crayon; art made with these crayons
tempera: process of painting in which paint is mixed with egg to produce a dull color
etching: art made by etching into a metal plate, putting ink on it, and pressing it to paper

P. 40
Answers will vary.

P. 43

Answers will vary. Students find two single cause-and-effect relationships and one multiple cause-and-effect relationship.
Possible answers:
Cause: The plane had to be fitted with a second gas tank.
Effect: There was no room for lights.;
Cause: There were no lights.
Effect: Ruth couldn't fly at night.;
Cause: Ruth couldn't fly at night.
Effect: She did not make it in one day.;
Cause with multiple effects: Ruth was a woman.
Effects: She got a smaller plane. She had to fly in a dress. She had difficulty getting her license.

P. 46

Answers may vary. Suggested answer:
Starting in any circle, but in this order:
Lightning, farmers, or bacteria put nitrogen into the soil.
Plants get nitrogen from soil, and animals get nitrogen from plants or other animals.
Plants and animals die and decay into the soil.
Bacteria changes the decayed matter back into nitrogen.

P. 49

Flowchart should be completed in this order:
Start.
Mix cookies according to recipe.
Put spoonfuls of dough on tray.
Put cookies in the oven.
Check cookies. Are they done?
Let cook a little longer.
Take cookies out of oven.
Stop.
Students' flowcharts will vary; check to see that they make sense.

P. 52

1. 6
2. 5
3. 33 feet
Student scores should appear this way on stem-and-leaf plot:
6 8 8 9 9
7 2 3 5 5 6
8 4 4 6 7 8 8 8
9 1 2 2 3 4 5 5 8

P. 55

Main Idea: Many animals protect themselves from predators by appearing to be something that they are not.
Details: Any detail from the rest of the paragraph.

P. 58

Note cards will vary.

P. 61

Outlines may vary.
Topic: Olympic games
  I. First Olympic games
    A. Held in Greece
    B. Only one race
    C. Only men allowed to participate
  II. Today's games
    A. Open to all athletes
    B. Olympic Committee chooses city
    C. Several thousand athletes in more than 20 sports
  III. Special Olympics
    A. Separate event
    B. People with disabilities compete
    C. They overcome challenges to have the Olympic experience

P. 64

1. 50
2. January
3. May
4. 370

P. 67

Graphs will vary.

P. 70

1. Ben and Anil
2. Crissy
3. 85
4. 360
5. Angelina

P. 73

Students' graphs will vary.

P. 76

New coordinates:
1. (6,9) (7,9) (7,8) (8,8) (8,6) (7,6) (7,5) (6,5)
2. (5,5) (7,5) (7,4) (6,4) (6,2) (7,2) (7,1) (5,1)
3. (4,4) (6,4) (5,2) (3,2)
Students' graphs will vary.

P. 79

1. 126
2. 104; 14
3. 20%
4. 40%; 56
5. Graphs should show the following:
   Small predators: 30%; 63 animals
   Cats: 40%; 84 animals
   Wolves and coyotes: 20%; 42 animals
   Birds: 10%; 21 animals

P. 82

1. 1776–1783
2. May, 1780
3. 7 years

P. 84

1. 600
2. 1,460
3. 3,000

P. 86

1. Hudson Bay and Hudson River
2. Students circle Baffin Bay and Baffin Island.
3. Sea of Cortés
4. Columbus, Ohio

P. 89

1. the Southwest
2. Nootka, Chinook, and Coos; Hunting and gathering and fishing
3. Farming and hunting and gathering
Students should label North America, South America, Antarctica, Asia, Australia, Europe, and Africa.

P. 91

Answers will vary.

P. 94

Vocabulary words and word cards will vary.